In Search of Ghosts

IN SEARCH
OF
GHOSTS

Daniel Cohen

Illustrated with photographs and reproductions

Dodd, Mead & Company · New York

ILLUSTRATION CREDITS

The illustrations in this book are used by permission and through the courtesy of the following: Milbourne Christopher Collection, 95; Culver Pictures, Inc., 78; John H. Cutten, 160, 172; Bruce Frisch, 60; Nathaniel Lieberman, ii; New York Public Library Picture Collection, 16, 17, 19, 25, 27, 28, 30, 56, 69, 93, 97, 138, 167; Dr. Paul Tabori, 144, 145. Photographs on pages 72 and 103 are from drawings by S. Drigin. Illustrations on pages 114 and 115 are from *Houdini on Magic* by Harry Houdini, Dover Publications, Inc., New York. Reprinted through permission of the publisher.

FRONTISPIECE: *A modern "spirit" photograph produced by trick photography.*

/33
C

ISBN: 0-396-06485-X
Library of Congress Catalog Card Number: 70-175312
Printed in the United States of America

To Fabian and Marlene

Acknowledgments

The author would like to express his thanks to John Cutten, Honorary Secretary of the British Society for Psychical Research, Gene Liberty of Creative Education Press, and Professor Rossell Hope Robbins, for their aid in obtaining photographs and drawings for this book.

Contents

INTRODUCTION

Do You Believe in Ghosts?

A fair question to ask anyone who sets out to write a book on ghosts is, "Do you believe in ghosts?"

I would have to give an answer that has been given many times before, "No, but I am afraid of them."

I have never seen or heard or otherwise experienced anything that I could reasonably consider a ghost. Naturally I have on occasion seen or heard or otherwise experienced things that I could and still cannot explain. But I have never had a good reason to attribute such "unexplained events" to ghosts.

The very existence of ghosts does not fit in with the modern scientific concept of the world. In fact, I am tempted to say that as far as I am concerned ghosts are simply impossible.

And yet, I would never willingly spend a night in a house that was reputed to be haunted. Graveyards make me nervous, even in the middle of the afternoon. And on a few occasions when I mistakenly thought that I had encountered a ghost, I have been as badly frightened as a person who did believe in them.

My most memorable encounter with a "ghost" took place just a few years ago. My wife and I visited England, and we were particularly anxious to see the ancient monument of Avebury.

11

Avebury is a huge circle of enormous stones, set up in prehistoric times. It is not nearly as well preserved or as famous as Stonehenge, which is only about twenty miles away, but it is much larger, and I think more impressive. In the middle of this ancient circle of stones is a small village built in medieval times.

The day we visited Avebury it was raining, as usual. My wife and I and an English friend were the only tourists at the monument. We walked around the circle discussing the dead and forgotten peoples who had labored to build such a tremendous structure. On a rainy day Avebury can make you feel pretty creepy, and the discussion soon proceeded to ghosts and other scary subjects.

After walking around the circle we went into the village. The largest house in the town was open to visitors for a small fee. It seemed a good place to get out of the rain for a while. I asked the girl collecting admissions if the house was supposed to be haunted. Most old houses in England are supposed to be haunted. She replied, matter of factly, that she didn't think that it was, but there were stories about a ghost having been seen in one of the rooms on the top floor.

As we wandered through the damp and deserted house, filled with furniture of another era and pictures of people long dead, the feeling of general unease grew. Finally we climbed to the upper story. "This is where the ghost is supposed to be," I said. Then I looked ahead and saw a woman in eighteenth-century dress seated with her back to me. At first I assumed that the figure was a dummy. And then the "dummy" stood up.

If I had a weak heart I probably would have had a heart attack. As it was, I just suffered a brief spasm of terror, before I realized that this eighteenth-century figure was no ghost, but a real living person. She was a costumed caretaker, whose job it

12

was to help show people around the house, and presumably make sure that they did not walk off with any of the valuables. It was a quiet day, and there were no other visitors. The care-taker had simply gone upstairs to rest and fallen asleep in her chair. The sound of my voice woke her up.

As I said, I don't believe in ghosts, but I am afraid of them. None of us can shake that lurking fear of ghosts, even when we are quite sure that such things do not exist. That is one of the reasons ghosts are so fascinating. For thousands of years telling ghost stories has been a popular form of entertainment. Just why we are entertained by things which frighten us I do not know, but that's how we are. Anything weird, horrible, and frightening is also fascinating to most of us.

No matter how rational we try to be, we just can't get rid of the feeling that perhaps ghost stories are not all fiction.

So fear is one reason why we search for ghosts; another is hope. These two attitudes seem contradictory, yet they exist side by side in our attitude toward ghosts. If there are such things as ghosts, that means that in some form or another man survives death. Friends and relatives who have died are not irrevocably separated from us. As ghosts, the dead have some form of contact with this world. The thought is very comforting. It is also very comforting to believe that we will somehow be able to influence, or at least observe, events on this earth after death.

This hope that the dead are never entirely separated from the living is a strong and almost overpowering emotion in some people. It is particularly strong among those who have recently lost a husband, wife, a parent or child, or a good friend.

So driven on by the two powerful emotions of fear and hope, we all search for ghosts in one way or another—even those of us who don't believe in them.

In this book we will look at mankind's efforts to get a definitive answer to the question "Are there such things as ghosts?" Though I have never been convinced by the evidence put forward for the existence of ghosts, I have always been intrigued by the search. Nor do I scorn all of those who do believe in ghosts. Certainly there have been a lot of fools and fakers who believed in ghosts, or said that they did. The most distasteful feature of the whole history of the search for ghosts is that it has attracted a large number of human vultures, who have preyed upon people's hopes and fears for their own personal gain. But the charlatans, while they have been part of the story, are by no means the whole story. There have been many intelligent and honest people who did believe in ghosts, and we will try to examine the evidence on which they based their beliefs. Some of this evidence is impressive; all of it is interesting.

Therefore, this is not to be a book of "ghost stories" in the usual sense of the term. You are not going to read works of fiction, or legends, or tales based solely on tradition and hearsay. This is to be a book of "real" or "true" ghost stories—that is, stories that people believed in at one time, and that many people still believe in today. I have tried to do the ghosts justice by presenting the best real ghost stories I could find, that is, those in which the evidence for the existence of ghosts seems soundest. Judge the evidence for yourself, and make up your own mind.

But before we try to figure out why some people believe in ghosts, and some people do not, we will look back at the time when everybody believed in them.

1

Man Meets Ghost

Men have always been afraid of the dead.

Even in prehistoric times the dead were treated with fearful awe. Often they were buried in deep graves which were covered by heavy stones, or by piles of smaller stones. These stones were not marks or signs of respect, they were signs of fear. They were meant to keep someone, or something, from getting out of the grave.

The dead can present the living with two sets of frightening problems. First, there are the problems concerning the corpse itself. Many people once believed—and some still do—that if a corpse is not properly attended to before it is buried it will rise up out of its grave and attack the living. Those in the greatest danger are the relatives of the dead man. They might be sought out by the vengeful dead for failing to take proper care of the corpse and thus causing it to wander about.

Another problem with corpses was that they seemed a bit like empty houses. They could always be taken over by someone, or something else. For a long time people believed that the air was filled with a host of wandering demons or spirits. These entities were invisible, and evil. What they craved most was a body that

15

Typical gravestones from early New England

they could inhabit. If one of these wandering demons happened to get inside a corpse the result was a monstrously evil, and dangerous, creature. So the period between the death of a man and the burial of his body was filled with peril.

Still, the corpse was a comparatively easy menace to deal with. It is, after all, a solid physical thing. Corpses could be kept in their graves by heavy stones or, in later times, by a heavy stone sarcophagus or a securely nailed coffin lid and six feet of earth. Some primitive peoples buried their dead tied up. The Egyptians wrapped their mummies in hundreds of yards of linen and even in modern times bodies were buried wrapped in winding sheets, perhaps a hang-over from the days in which a corpse was tied up in the grave.

Demons and evil spirits could be warded off by the appropriate spells and incantations, by rituals and the smell of incense, and by magic charms and figures. The best protection was to get the corpse buried quickly and properly. If a corpse was still restless after all the proper magical rites had been per-

16

formed it could be burned, and in any event it would rot away
after a few years and that would be an end to it.

A ghost represented a more perplexing and persistent problem.

A belief in, and fear of, ghosts is perfectly natural and logical. When a man dies he becomes a corpse. That is obvious
enough. But it is also quite obvious that something is missing.
A corpse, though it may look like a living man, lacks a soul,
spirit, personality, life force, or what have you. This "thing"
that apparently has departed from the corpse at death has been
called by many different names. But whatever it was called, it
was that which gave the physical body movement, feeling, intelligence—in short, gave it life. This spirit was easily as important as the body itself, and quite probably more important.
Just because you couldn't see it did not mean it didn't exist.
Primitive man was very logical. He reasoned that the spirit
could not simply disappear because it no longer inhabited the
body. It had to go somewhere. But where?

For most of his history, man has believed in magic. In a pre-

*In ancient Peru the mummies of the dead were carefully tied up, per-
haps to keep them from walking away.*

17

scientific society magic makes perfectly good sense. One of the principles of magic is that things that have once been together always retain some sort of magical link with one another. Thus in the case of ghosts the spirit which had once been inside the body was still somehow connected with it after death. The most obvious connection was that the spirit or ghost was hovering near the remains of the body from which it had been separated. That is why graveyards were, and still are, considered such frightening places. The spirits of all those people buried in the graveyard might be hanging around.

If we follow this magical logic one step further we can see that what happened to a corpse would matter a great deal to its ghost. This was another important reason for carefully burying the dead.

But the ghost need not necessarily stay near the body it had inhabited in life. A ghost might be connected with some spot in which the living person had spent a lot of time—the house that he had lived in, for example. Another place for the ghost to hover would be the place where the person had met his death. Or there might be a special place in the universe for ghosts or spirits. In a primitive society this could be a cave, a dark forest, or any other appropriately gloomy spot. Any place that acquired such a reputation would usually be avoided at all costs.

Primitive man was also profoundly conservative—he didn't like any change. Any interruption in what seemed to be the natural order of things was looked upon with great foreboding. There was the world of the living, and there was the world of the dead—that was how things should be. If beings from these two worlds got mixed up with one another then something terrible might happen, usually to the living. Any ghost was a thing to be feared. A man who had been good and kind in life might still

18

The fifteenth-century magician, Edward Kelly, and his associate raise a dead person.

make a very dangerous ghost. An evil man was to be feared more in death than in life.

Not everybody held the same attitude toward ghosts. Some people treated them fairly casually while others were almost paralyzed with fear at the mere mention of the subject of ghosts. Some societies worshipped the ghosts of their ancestors. But in general ghosts were not popular, and most people preferred to avoid them whenever and however possible.

Men developed a vast number of customs and rituals to keep from arousing the dead—to keep the ghosts in their place. One of the most common methods of not disturbing the dead was simply not to mention the name of anyone who had recently died. The ghost of the newly dead man was usually considered stronger and closer than the ghost of one who had died long ago. If the nearby ghost hears his name he might answer to it, and the results would probably be disagreeable, to say the least.

Sir James Frazer, whose book *The Golden Bough* was a pioneer study of folklore and custom, collected scores of examples of different peoples who feared to mention the name of the dead. This is one of the incidents he cites. There was a Mr. Oldfield who was studying the aborigines of Australia.

"Once Mr. Oldfield so terrified a native by shouting out the name of a deceased person that the man fairly took to his heels and did not venture to show himself for several days. At their next meeting he bitterly reproached the rash white man for his indiscretion; 'nor could I,' adds Mr. Oldfield, 'induce him by any means to utter the awful sound of the dead man's name, for by so doing he would have placed himself in the power of the malign spirit.' "

In other tribes, says Frazer, all those people who have names similar to that of the dead man will change their names, lest the ghost become confused and answer to the wrong name.

A trace of this very same fear can be found all around us even today. At funerals many people will not utter the name of the person who has died. Rather they speak of "the departed," "the deceased," or even "the loved one." When they do mention the name of the dead their voice drops to near a whisper. Unconsciously perhaps they feel that if they speak softly the ghost will not hear them.

Not everybody in ancient times lived in overpowering fear of the spirits of the dead, however. The ancient Greeks believed that the spirits of the dead were consigned to a dismal and shadowy sort of underworld. In fact, one of the earliest, and still one of the best, ghost stories we have concerns a man who visited the land of the dead.

The story appears in Homer's *Odyssey* written somewhere around the year 700 B.C. The hero Odysseus wanted to know when he would finally return home from his wanderings. He was told to descend into the underworld and question the ghost of the great prophet Tiresias.

When Odysseus reached the gloomy twilight world, the phantoms of the dead crowded around him, but were so weak and insubstantial that they hardly had the strength to speak. Odysseus dug a pit and filled it with the blood of sacrificed animals, but he had to keep the ghosts at bay with his sword until the spirit of Tiresias appeared to drink first.

The lot of these Greek ghosts was a miserable one. The great hero Achilles, now a spirit, mournfully informs Odysseus, "I had rather be a poor man's serf than king over all of the dead."

Still, not all of the Greeks were thoroughly convinced that the spirits of the dead were safely stowed away in the underworld. Nor did all Greeks contemplate confronting ghosts with the calm

21

Odysseus holds back the spirits of the dead.

assurance of an Odysseus. Greek soldiers would sometimes cut the feet off of enemies they had slain in battle. The hope was that the crippled ghost would be unable to pursue its killer effectively.

Certainly the best way to assure that the spirits of the dead would rest easy and not trouble the living was to make sure that bodies were properly buried. While in the underworld Odysseus met the ghost of one of his sailors who had been killed, but whose corpse had not been buried. The ghost warned Odysseus not to tempt the wrath of the gods by allowing his corpse to remain unburied. The Greeks and most other ancient peoples would go to great lengths to make sure that their dead were properly interred. One of the greatest of all Greek plays concerns the efforts of Antigone to obtain a proper burial for the remains of her brother.

Educated and sophisticated Greeks, those who attended the theater, were probably not directly concerned with ghosts. They thought that if the dead had not been properly buried this would offend the gods and bring ill luck, perhaps disaster. But such beliefs originated in a simple fear of ghosts. And the common people still feared the wrath of the wandering spirit of an unburied dead man.

If anything, the Romans were more afraid of ghosts than were the Greeks. Even the educated often took the subject quite seriously. One of the earliest "true" ghost stories in existence was written nearly 2,000 years ago by a man called Pliny the Younger. Pliny was no ignorant and superstitious fool. He was highly cultured and educated, and one of the foremost orators and writers of his day. In addition, he was the nephew of another man named Pliny who was Rome's greatest natural scientist. Pliny the Younger, like his uncle, did not like to accept

23

hearsay evidence and was skeptical about many of the things he was told. Yet he was impressed by a ghost story he had heard and was ready to vouch for the truth of it. He told the story in a letter to his rich friend and patron, Lucias Sura.

"There was formerly at Athens a large and handsome house which none the less had acquired the reputation of being badly haunted. The folk told how at the dead of night horrid noises were heard: the clanking of chains which grew louder and louder until there suddenly appeared the hideous phantom of an old man who seemed the very picture of abject filth and misery. His beard was long and matted, his white hair dishevelled and unkempt. His thin legs were loaded with a weight of galling fetters that he dragged wearily along with a painful moaning; his wrists were shackled by long cruel links, whilst ever and anon he raised his arms and shook his shackles in a kind of impotent fury. Some few mocking skeptics who were once bold enough to watch all night in the house had been well-nigh scared from their senses at the sight of the apparition; and, what was worse, disease and even death itself proved the fate of those who after dusk had ventured within those accursed walls. The place was shunned. A placard 'To Let' was posted, but year succeeded year and the house fell almost to ruin and decay."

Then, according to Pliny, the philosopher Athenodorus visited the city, looking for a house to rent. Like most philosophers he was not a rich man. He was looking for a house that would rent cheaply. He spied the dilapidated old house with its "To Let" sign, and inquired how much the rent would be. "Being not a little surprised at the low figure asked, he put more questions, and then there came out the whole story." But the philosopher decided to rent the house anyway.

It was Athenodorus' habit to write and study at night, and on

A "ghastly figure" appears to the philosopher Athenodorus.

his first night in the haunted house he refused to change his routine. In fact, he decided to work on some particularly difficult problems, so that his mind would be fully absorbed and would not play tricks on him, and make him see things that were not there.

"He was soon absorbed in philosophical calculations, but presently the noise of a rattling chain, at first distant and then growing nearer, broke on his ear. However, Athenodorus, being particularly occupied with his notes, was too intent to interrupt his writings until, as the clanking became more and more continuous, he looked up, and there before him stood the phantom exactly as he had been described.

"The ghastly figure seemed to beckon with its finger, but the philosopher signed with his hand that he was busy, and again bent to his writing. The chains were shaken angrily and with per-

25

sistence, upon which Athenodorus quietly arose from his seat, and, taking the lamp, motioned the spectre to lead before."

The ghost led the philosopher through the house and into a garden. At a spot in the garden shrubbery the ghost signed and disappeared. Athenodorus marked the spot, and then went back into the house and retired for the night. He slept soundly. The next morning he went to the local magistrates, told them what he had seen and suggested that the spot at which the ghost had disappeared should be investigated. This was done, and when the investigators started digging they unearthed a human skeleton just a few feet below the surface. Ancient and rusted chains still clung to the bones. The remains were carefully collected and properly buried. The house was then cleansed by various rituals, and it was never again troubled by ghosts or bad luck.

This story, though it was first told nearly twenty centuries ago sounds surprisingly modern. The image of the chain-rattling ghost has reappeared regularly through the years, sometimes in fictional ghost stories (remember Marley's ghost in Dickens' *A Christmas Carol*) and other times in ghost stories that were supposed to be true.

The chain-rattling ghost tradition provoked a rather humorous comment from Captain Francis Grose, an eighteenth-century antiquarian who wrote a tongue-in-cheek pamphlet on the characteristics of ghosts. "Dragging chains is not the fashion of English ghosts, chains and black vestments being chiefly the accoutrements of foreign spectres, seen in arbitrary governments; dead or alive, English spirits are free."

In this ancient ghost story, as well as in most modern ones, the ghost appears just as the living man had appeared when he died, or shortly thereafter. The traditional ghost wears a white sheet because at one time it was customary to bury corpses in

26

Marley's ghost appears to Scrooge, from Charles Dickens' story, A Christmas Carol.

white winding sheets. Today corpses are buried in ordinary clothes, but the image of the white-sheeted ghost lingers on.

Another rather modern sounding feature of this ancient story is that the ghost had a mission. Ghosts in modern times don't wander about just to scare people; they usually have something

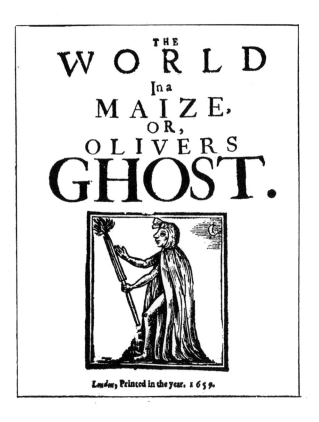

Title page from a ghost story published in 1659. Ghost is shown in traditional winding sheet.

that they want done. In this case the ghost seemed to wish to insure that his remains received a proper burial.

The ancient Greeks and Romans were pagans. They saw the world as being filled with a huge variety of gods and spirits. In such a world ghosts would not seem out of place. But for the fiercely monotheistic Hebrews, belief in ghosts presented more of a problem. To the Hebrews the Lord was all-powerful—all things good and evil came from Him. In such a tight and well-ordered world it was much harder to believe that the spirits of the dead could just walk the earth seeking vengeance or doing

28

whatever else it was that ghosts were supposed to do.

Of course, many of the Hebrews still believed in ghosts anyway. This belief was much too ancient and too deep to be cast off completely. But it was considered unorthodox to believe in ghosts and people didn't talk much about them.

There is little mention of ghosts or spirits in the Old Testament. Since ghosts don't really fit in with a concept of a single all-powerful God, they had to be regarded as ungodly and therefore evil. Thus anyone who had any dealings with ghosts or spirits was performing an unnatural and an ungodly act, for which he was sure to suffer.

The most celebrated "ghost story" in the Bible recounts just such a case; and reveals much about the ancient Hebrew attitude toward ghosts, and people who dealt with them.

King Saul of Israel was facing a battle with his enemies, the Philistines. He was not at all sure what the outcome of the battle would be. "And when Saul enquired of the Lord, the Lord answered him not, neither by dreams . . . nor prophets."

So Saul determined to try another method of finding out how the battle would go—necromancy—questioning the dead about the future. Traditionally the dead were supposed to be able to foresee coming events. Most of the other peoples of the ancient Middle East regularly attempted necromancy. The Babylonians had a whole class of priests who specialized in the subject. But to the Hebrews such attempts to "get around" God were both evil and dangerous.

However, King Saul felt desperate and so was willing to make the attempt. He went to visit a woman called the Witch of Endor, and asked her to summon up the spirit of the prophet Samuel. The woman was very wary, because King Saul had previously banned all attempts at conversing with the dead, and other acts of

29

The apparition of Samuel appearing to King Saul.

sorcery, on pain of death. But Saul assured the Witch of Endor that she would not be punished. So she conjured up the spirit of Samuel, "An old man . . . covered with a mantle."

The old prophet was not at all happy about having been summoned in such an ungodly manner. "Why hast thou disquieted me, to bring me up?" he demanded. King Saul explained that the Lord would no longer answer his questions, but he thought that Samuel might.

That made Samuel even angrier. "Wherefore then dost thou ask of me, seeing the Lord is departed from thee, and is become thine enemy?"

Samuel did issue a prophecy, but it was a grim and terrible one. Not only would the Israelites lose to the Philistines but Saul and his sons would die as a result of the battle. The next day the demoralized King Saul led his army to defeat. His sons were killed in the battle and in despair Saul killed himself with his own sword.

There is really no place in the Christian world for ghosts either. The souls of the dead are supposed to go to heaven or to hell. They are not supposed to be lurking about drafty castle halls, clanking chains and moaning. But, as usual, people could not shake their ancient belief in the apparitions and spirits and the like. They just tried to explain the existence of such things a little differently.

Since the ghost was clearly an unnatural creature, one which defied God's orderly world, it had to be a creation of the Devil. In the minds of many Christians ghosts became not so much a spirit of the dead, but rather some sort of demon or evil spirit sent up by Satan himself to frighten, mislead, or tempt man. This demon could take any shape, including that of a man who had died.

31

Even the raising of the spirit of Samuel, as described in the Bible, was reinterpreted from this viewpoint. One sixteenth-century theologian contended that Samuel was not raised from the dead. ". . . It was an illusion or cozenage practiced by the witch . . ." Others insisted that a demon or the Devil himself had assumed the form of the spirit of Samuel.

Many of those strange, odd, frightening, or inexplicable occurrences that once might have been attributed to ghosts came to be attributed to the terrible practice of witchcraft.

For nearly three hundred years—from the middle of the fifteenth century to nearly the end of the seventeenth century—much of Europe was gripped by a hysterical fear of witchcraft. The witch hysteria touched colonial America, and in 1692 Salem, Massachusetts, was the scene of the last major witchcraft trials in the world. During the centuries of persecution hundreds of thousands, perhaps millions, of innocent people were tortured and killed on the charge of witchcraft. During this period, most people didn't have time to worry about ghosts.

By the beginning of the eighteenth century the witchcraft hysteria had died down, and ghost stories were again used to account for unusual and apparently supernatural happenings. The case of Major Thomas Weir of Scotland illustrates the transformation of a witchcraft tale into a good ghost story.

During the seventeenth century Major Weir was one of Edinburgh's most upstanding citizens. He was regarded as a man of undisputed honesty and fierce, almost fanatical, religious piety. He was the last person in Edinburgh that anyone would have suspected of witchcraft. Then in the year 1670, when Major Weir was some seventy years old, he suddenly confessed to a long series of crimes, including witchcraft.

For two centuries the Scots had been particularly obsessed

with witchcraft. People were regularly tortured and burned with little or no evidence to support the charge. But Weir had been such a righteous man that at first no one would believe his confession. They thought he had gone mad, and they were probably right. But Major Weir persisted in confessing to witchcraft and some doctors examined him and adjudged him to be sane. He was brought to trial and executed along with his sister who was also implicated in the crimes.

Because of Major Weir's standing in the community his case became very famous. But it also took place when the witchcraft mania was beginning to die down. Yet the Weir case remained

Edinburgh home of the notorious Major Thomas Weir in The Bow

famous long after people stopped believing in witchcraft. The gloomy Weir house on the street called The Bow in Edinburgh became the center for what was reputed to be all sorts of weird and ghostly activity.

People reported seeing spectral coaches drive to the door of the house in order to take the Major and his sister to hell. No one would live in the place and it remained vacant for a century. Finally one old couple was induced to move in because of the low rent. The next morning they fled, swearing that a calf had gazed at them while they were in bed. (Just why this should have frightened them so has not been recorded.) The house remained empty and falling into ruin until 1830 when it was finally torn down. During this entire period it may well have been the most famous haunted house in the entire world.

A book called *Traditions of Edinburgh*, published in 1825, says, "His [Major Weir's] house, though known to be deserted by everything human, was sometimes observed at midnight to be full of lights, and heard to emit strange sounds as of dancing, howling, and what is strangest of all, spinning. Some people occasionally saw the Major issue from the low close at midnight, mounted on a black horse without a head, and gallop off in a whirlwind of flame."

Shortly before the house was torn down the novelist Sir Walter Scott testified to the hold it retained on the popular imagination:

"Bold was the urchin from the high school who dared approach the gloomy ruin at the risk of seeing the Major's enchanted staff parading through the old apartments, or hearing the hum of the necromantic wheel, which procured for his sister such a character as a spinner."

Thus a man who in his own time had been condemned as a

witch was transformed into the central character in a tale of ghosts and haunted houses, because people no longer believed in witchcraft.

But the very same doubts that had been raised about witchcraft were now being raised about ghosts. People no longer asked whether ghosts were really spirits of the dead or illusions of the Devil. For the first time in history a large number of people began to wonder whether ghosts were not just illusions produced by the human imagination.

Now, of course, most people continued to believe in ghosts. They shunned the Weir house and other houses that had the reputation for being haunted. There were so many tales of ghosts that to doubt them seemed foolish. It seemed to fly in the face of an overwhelming mass of evidence. And yet the doubters multiplied. Most of the doubt was caused by the rise of science. Ghosts didn't fit in with the picture of the natural world that was being developed by scientists. Ghosts were even more out of place in the naturalistic world of the eighteenth century than they had been in the concept of the world developed by the early Jews and Christians.

Even more pressing was the problem of evidence. Science laid great stress upon evidence—on what sort of facts there were to support any particular belief. Ghosts couldn't be taken into a laboratory and measured. Nor could they be observed with a telescope or a microscope. The evidence was made up entirely of what persons had said they had seen or otherwise experienced.

As it turned out, while everybody seemed to know some stories about ghosts, relatively few claimed to have seen or directly to have experienced them. For example, no reputable people could be found who would give firsthand testimony that they had seen Major Weir ride off on a headless horse. Plenty of persons claimed to have heard strange noises issuing from the house, but there are many explanations for strange noises that do not involve ghosts.

Some people said that they had heard about a particular ghost directly from the person who had seen it. But more commonly the ghost story was told by someone who had heard it from someone else, who may have heard it from yet another person, and so on. As far as scientific evidence was concerned the whole mass of ghost stories just didn't count for very much.

Sir Walter Scott loved a ghost story, but he was very cautious about accepting the literal truth of any of these stories. He advised that we all adopt the attitude of a particular English judge. "The judge stopped a witness who was about to give the account of the murder upon trial, as it was narrated to him by the ghost of the murdered person. 'Hold, sir,' said his lordship; 'the ghost is an excellent witness, and his evidence the best possible; but he cannot be heard by proxy in this court. Summon him hither, and I'll hear him in person; but your communication is mere hearsay, which my office compels me to reject.' "

Scott continues, "Yet it is upon the credit of a man, who pledges it upon that of three or four persons who have told it successively to each other, that we are often expected to believe an incident inconsistent with the laws of nature, however agreeable to our love of the wonderful and the horrible."

If we are to pursue *real* ghosts rather than just start telling ghost stories we will have to concentrate on those accounts which have been documented or investigated. In the next chapter we will look at some classic *real* ghost stories.

2

Real Ghost Stories

Now *real* ghosts—and by that I mean ghosts for whose existence there is more than hearsay evidence—rarely fit the stereotype of the traditional ghost of fiction. The ghost of Anne Boleyn, one of Henry VIII's unfortunate wives, was supposed to have been seen walking the corridors of the Tower of London with her severed head tucked underneath her arm. She is the sort of ghost who makes a dandy story, but unfortunately (or fortunately, depending on your attitude toward ghosts) there isn't much evidence to support this story.

Nor is there much good evidence in behalf of the hordes of ghostly knights and pale ladies who apparently inhabit every old castle and house in England, Scotland, and Wales. The ghost of Abraham Lincoln, which is supposed to haunt the White House, the transparent southern belles, and the spectral Indian chiefs of America are likewise without much foundation in hard evidence.

Real ghosts, or rather real ghostly events, are far more varied than the sight of an apparition floating up and down a corridor. Here are some of the classic cases in the annals of real ghost stories.

THE DRUMMER OF TEDWORTH

Probably the first ghost story that was ever investigated objectively concerned a strange sort of ghost—practically not a ghost at all. The case was called The Drummer of Tedworth.

It began in the town of Tedworth, England, in March of 1662. A traveling showman named William Drury was arrested for using counterfeit documents. The local magistrate, John Mompesson, set Drury free, but confiscated his drum. Drury had once been a drummer in the army and he considered the drum a vital part of his act. He was very attached to it, and quite upset when it was taken away from him. Within a few days all manner of strange things began to occur at the Mompesson house.

The house was assailed by a loud drumming sound which grew worse after Drury's confiscated drum was destroyed. The Mompesson children were lifted out of bed by an unseen hand. At night the covers were torn off Mr. Mompesson's bed, and his shoes were thrown at him. Other objects in the house were thrown around. Books were hidden, chamberpots were emptied onto beds, and, in general, life in the Mompesson house became very uncomfortable.

All of this was very strange, to be sure. But you might argue that there is little evidence of any ghost here. One servant was terrified by the vision of "a Great Body with two red and glaring eyes." The people of the time thought that the cause of the disturbances was witchcraft. However, these events, the noises, the moving objects, and so forth would today be classed as poltergeist phenomena. "Poltergeist" is a German word which means "noisy spirit." People who investigate strange occurrences today are called psychical researchers. They investigate poltergeists as well as investigating ghosts and hauntings. The various events seem to overlap with one another and the techniques for investi-

Joseph Glanvill (1636-1680), the earliest psychical researcher

gating the different types of phenomena are pretty much the same.

A second reason for looking at The Drummer of Tedworth case is that it attracted the attention of Joseph Glanvill. Glanvill was an intelligent, educated, and important man. He was chaplin to King Charles II of England. Glanville believed implicitly in witchcraft, as did most of the men of his day. In fact, he was an active investigator of witchcraft. But unlike most other witch hunters, he was neither a fool nor a monster. He really tried to establish the facts of the case against an accused witch, and not be swept along by superstition and hysteria. Joseph Glanvill might be classed as the father of modern psychical research, and the case of The Drummer of Tedworth as the first attempt at a serious investigation of psychic phenomena.

Glanvill traveled to Tedworth to question the witness firsthand. He himself was witness to some of the strange events, though they were not as spectacular as the "Great Body with two red and glaring eyes." While investigating the case one of Mompesson's maids told him "it was come." He hurried up to one of the bedrooms. "There were two little modest Girls in the Bed, between seven and eleven Years old, as I guest." Glanvill heard a scratching in the bed "as loud as one with long Nails could make upon a Bolster." This went on for about half an hour and was followed by a noise which sounded like a dog panting. There was also some movement in the bedding. He published his evidence and conclusions in a book, and provided us with our first complete account of the investigation of a poltergeist. Some of the stories he recorded sound incredible, yet believable.

"On the fifth of November, 1662, it [the Drummer] kept a mighty noise, and a servant observing two boards in the children's room seeming to move, he bid it give him one of them. Upon which the board came (nothing moving it that he saw) within a yard of him. The man added, 'Nay, let me have it in my hand.' Upon which, it was shoved quite home to him. He thrust it back and it was driven to him again, and so up and down, to and fro, at least twenty times together, till Mr. Mompesson forbade his servant such familiarities. This was in the daytime, and seen by a whole room full of people . . ."

Glanvill reported many similar marvelous events at the Mompesson house. The obvious explanation seemed to be that the angry drummer, William Drury, had somehow bewitched the house. Early in 1663 Drury was again arrested in a nearby town. The charge was not witchcraft, but pig stealing. He was found guilty and sentenced to be transported to the American colonies. But he escaped from the convict ship and made his way

Illustration from Glanvill's Saducismus Triumphatus *(1683), showing six devilish happenings. Box in upper left illustrates the Drummer of Tedworth case, which Glanvill himself investigated.*

to a town just a few miles from Tedworth. He bought another drum, and began beating it in the town square. Within twenty-four hours Magistrate Mompesson had him arrested on the charge of witchcraft.

Drury apparently did confess to, or rather boast of, causing the disturbances at the Mompesson house, though he did not say how. He was acquitted on the charge of witchcraft anyway. On the original charge of pig stealing, however, he was condemned to transportation to the colonies, and this time he did not escape.

What happened at Tedworth in 1662? What caused the mysterious drummings and all the other strange disturbances? We can rule out the idea of witchcraft, because we no longer believe in witchcraft. We are then left with two explanations: Either the phenomena were caused by a poltergeist, or someone was playing an elaborate and rather nasty joke on Magistrate Mompesson.

We must repeat that Glanvill was no superstitious fool. He certainly considered the idea of trickery. While he was asking questions someone told him that the disturbances had been caused by "two young women in the house with a design to scare thence Mr. Mompesson's mother." But Glanvill rejected the idea of trickery. He didn't think that any human being, or group of human beings could possibly have been responsible for all of the strange happenings. He also could discover no possible motives for such trickery. "And what interest could any of his [Mompesson's] family have had (if it had been possible to have managed it without discovery) to continue so long and so troublesome and so injurious an imposture?"

Glanvill's reasoning is perfectly sound, as far as it goes. But we cannot rule out trickery so easily. People who want to play tricks can be very malicious and very ingenious. Glanvill recorded a couple of incidents which should have made him more suspicious. Every once in a while a member of the household would become so enraged at "the Drummer" that he would pick up a weapon and charge at the source of the disturbance. This sort of show of force always made the disturbance cease.

Once Mompesson himself saw some wood move in a chimney room and grabbed a pistol and fired at the moving wood. Later, blood was found nearby on the stairs, and in other places in the house. Ghosts do not usually bleed.

But no one ever confessed to faking The Drummer of Tedworth phenomena. If trickery was involved all the events certainly could not have taken place exactly as described. But were the descriptions accurate? We don't really know. People usually do tend to exaggerate the strangeness of strange events that they have experienced. The King himself sent a special committee to investigate the phenomena, but they did not see or hear anything unusual at Tedworth.

So there it is. After nearly three hundred years we are not going to be able to solve the mystery. Poltergeist or trickery? You can make up your own mind.

THE DEVIL OF WOODSTOCK

A few years before the incident at Tedworth there had been an even more spectacular series of events at a house in Woodstock, Oxfordshire, England. The year was 1649, and King Charles I had just been beheaded by a rebellious Parliament. A committee was sent to strip the dead king's manor house in Oxfordshire of everything of value. Almost immediately, after the commission arrived at the house, all sorts of strange and violent things began to happen. There was a succession of loud noises. Bricks came flying through windows. Dishes and pots

43

were thrown at the commissioners, and buckets of "green stinking water" drenched them when they tried to sleep.

One of the commissioners saw the hoof of a strange animal—or was it a demon? He drew his sword and was immediately knocked unconscious.

After King Charles' descendants regained the throne a man who was known to his friends as "Funny Joe" confessed to having been "the good devil of Woodstock." "Funny Joe," it seems, was a fanatic Royalist, who joined the rebel commission under an assumed name. With the aid of a couple of like-minded friends he had staged all the ghostly effects.

THE GREEN GHOST OF VAUVERT

Not all ghosts or, for that matter, all tricksters are English. In the mid-thirteenth century the very pious King Louis IX of France gave a house near Paris to six monks from the Order of St. Bruno. However, from the window of their new house the monks could see a much finer residence nearby. It was the palace of Vauvert. The palace had been built by King Robert as a royal residence but had been unused for many years.

Vauvert, though deserted, never had the reputation of being haunted until the monks of St. Bruno became its neighbors. From then on, frightful shrieks and howlings were heard from the palace practically every night. People reported seeing strange lights in the windows. Finally a huge green spectre with a long white beard was seen regularly at an upstairs window howling and shaking his fist at passers-by.

The stories of the ghostly or diabolical goings on at Vauvert soon reached the ears of the king, who was shocked, and sent a commission to investigate. The monks of St. Bruno also professed to be shocked, but they hinted to the commissioners that if they were allowed to inhabit the palace they would soon expel the ghost.

The King was relieved and delighted to hear that the monks offered to undertake the dangerous task of getting rid of the ghost. A deed was soon drawn up making the palace of Vauvert the property of the monks of St. Bruno. The disturbances ended immediately.

Was there really a ghost or evil spirit haunting the palace of Vauvert? Were the monks able to drive it away? Or did they stage the entire haunting in order to obtain a nice piece of property for their order? As always, you can make up your own mind—because there is no solid proof one way or the other. But since the monks had such a very good reason for haunting Vauvert themselves, and a splendid opportunity to do so, it seems fairly safe to assume that the haunting of Vauvert is another case of trickery.

The Cock Lane Ghost

Trickery was easy enough at Vauvert and Woodstock, for those cases were not really closely investigated. Even in the Drummer of Tedworth case the investigation was minimal. But by the eighteenth century the investigators of ghosts had really begun to close in. People in general no longer feared and shunned ghosts as they once had. On the contrary, many people seemed downright anxious to meet up with a ghost. So in 1762 when the rumor got around London that there was a ghost haunting a house in an obscure little street called Cock Lane, people jammed into the street hoping to get a glimpse of the ghost, or at least to see the haunted house.

The supposedly haunted house was owned by a man named Parsons. The ghost was that of a Miss Fanny, distant relative

Cock Lane, scene of one of the most celebrated ghost stories of all times

of a stockbroker named Kent who rented the Cock Lane property from Parsons. Miss Fanny had come to serve as Kent's housekeeper (some said mistress) after his wife died.

Kent and Parsons quarreled about money. Kent moved out

and sued his former landlord. At about this time, Miss Fanny died. The official verdict was that the death had been caused by smallpox, but Parson hinted rather darkly that Miss Fanny had been poisoned by Kent.

There the matter rested for approximately two years. Then at the beginning of 1762 the area around Cock Lane was alive with the news that the Parsons' house was being haunted by the ghost of poor dead Fanny. Elizabeth Parsons, daughter of the owner of the house and a girl of about twelve, said that she had actually seen the ghost and that the ghost informed her that she had been poisoned. No one else reported seeing the ghost, but many persons heard loud and mysterious knockings and scratchings. The ghost was tagged with the nickname, "Scratching Fanny."

According to Elizabeth, the ghost would not render herself visible to anyone else, but she would answer questions by a simple knocking code, one knock for yes, two for no. Scratching indicated displeasure.

The possibility of a ghost answering questions was taken quite seriously. A committee headed by several clergymen decided to sit up all night in the Parsons' house in order to interrogate the ghost. Here are some of the questions they asked. The answers were delivered by a knock or knocks:

"Do you make this disturbance on account of the ill-usage you received from Mr. Kent?"—"Yes."

"Were you brought to an untimely end by poison?"—"Yes."

A former servant of Fanny named Carrots was present at the interrogation. The ghost was asked, "Can your former servant, Carrots, give any information about the poison?"—"Yes."

"How long before your death did you tell your servant, Carrots, that you were poisoned? An hour?"—"Yes."

Carrots was appealed to, but she said she knew nothing of

47

poison, and that Fanny had been quite unable to speak an hour before her death. That shook the faith of some of the investigators, but the interrogation continued.

"If Mr. Kent is arrested for this murder, will he confess?"—"Yes."

"Would your soul be at rest if he were hanged for it?"—"Yes."

"Will he be hanged for it?"—"Yes."

When word of this conversation with the dead got around, little Cock Lane was overflowing with curiosity seekers. Parsons began charging admission to get in to see his haunted house. Everyone in London, even the great Dr. Samuel Johnson, discussed the case of the Cock Lane ghost with great interest and gravity.

One of the investigators, the Reverend Mr. Aldritch of Clerkenwell, was pastor of St. John's Church, where the body of the dead woman was deposited in a vault. The ghost promised Mr. Aldritch that she would follow Elizabeth Parsons to the church vault and give notice of her presence by a distinct knock upon her coffin lid.

A large party of ladies and gentlemen gathered at Mr. Aldritch's house near the church. The girl was brought to the house and at about 10 o'clock she was put to bed. The men were getting ready to go down into the vault when a great commotion erupted in the girl's room. The girl said that the ghost had arrived. The ladies who were in the room with her affirmed that they had heard the now familiar knocks and scratchings.

But Mr. Aldritch was a hard and suspicious man. He ordered the girl to take her hands out from under the covers, and he held them firmly while he questioned the ghost. There were no answers. Finally he asked the ghost to make its presence known by

The "ghost's" house in Cock Lane

any sign—touching the cheek or hand of someone in the room, rustling the curtains, any sign at all. Nothing happened.

Still the men decided to go through with the second part of the experiment. At about midnight they all went down into the vault and took up positions alongside Fanny's coffin. Here is how one chronicle described the scene: "The ghost was then summoned to appear, but it appeared not; it was summoned to knock, but it knocked not; it was summoned to scratch, but it scratched not." Many of those who left the vault after the failure of this test were convinced that they had been hoaxed by Parsons and his daughter.

49

Others did not want to be hasty. They wished to remain open-minded. Perhaps the ghost was offended by the rough and the rather skeptical treatment it had received. They decided that if the ghost of Fanny was to answer anyone, she would surely answer Kent, her accused murderer. It was in order to see Kent hanged that the ghost had presumably become restless in the first place. So Kent was brought to the vault and he loudly asked the ghost whether he had indeed murdered her. Again nothing happened.

Still there were those who continued to defend the reality of the Cock Lane ghost. The rumor spread that Kent had Fanny's body removed from its coffin before the test, so that the ghost would be unable to appear. So Kent had the coffin opened in front of a group of witnesses who confirmed that the body was indeed there.

By now the long-suffering Kent had reached the end of his rope. He brought suit against Parsons, his wife, a servant in the house, and a printer whom they had hired to publish an account of the haunting. The trial was held on July 10, 1762, and the judge, Lord Chief Justice Mansfield, not only found all the defendants guilty, and meted out stiff sentences, he also severely reprimanded the minister who carried out the first investigation of "Scratching Fanny."

Parsons and his associates maintained their innocence throughout the trial. The prosecution was never able to explain how the entire deception had been accomplished. In one instance Elizabeth Parsons was found to have concealed a block of wood under her dress and knocked on it. But this did not explain all the noises. So at least a few continued to believe in the ghost of "Scratching Fanny." Even today she still has her supporters among psychical researchers.

There is a curious little footnote to this case. Some years after the Cock Lane excitement had died down, a man named J. W. Archer visited the crypt of St. John's Church at Clerkenwell where the body of "Scratching Fanny" was entombed. At the time the interior of the vault was in great confusion. He sat down upon a coffin which the sexton's boy, who was holding the lantern for him, said belonged to "Scratching Fanny." Remembering the Cock Lane case, Archer was very curious. He pried the lid off the coffin, "and saw the face of a handsome woman, with an aquiline nose; this feature remaining perfect, an uncommon case, for the cartilage mostly gives way." The rest of the remains were also "perfectly preserved."

Archer saw no trace of smallpox, the disease which was supposed to have killed Fanny. He also recalled that some mineral poisons help to preserve bodies.

"I made particular inquiries at the time of Mr. Bird, churchwarden, a respectable and judicious man; and he gave me good assurance that the coffin had always been looked upon as the one containing the Cock Lane woman."

While the whole Cock Lane ghost business seems to have been a fraud, the case still leaves one with a slightly eerie and unsure feeling.

BEALINGS BELLS

The ghostly bells that "were not rung by any mortal hand" are a standard feature of many supernatural stories. In fact, there are quite a number of cases in which this sort of thing was actually supposed to have happened. The most well-documented, and oldest of all, is the case of the Bealings Bells.

On February 2, 1834, the bells in the house of Major Edward Moor at Great Bealings, Suffolk, began to ring violently, without any apparent cause. The bells were in the kitchen, and wires led to bell pulls in different rooms. The purpose of the bells was to alert the servants that they were wanted. The servants knew which room the call had come from, by seeing which bell rang. Major Moor, who was retired from the Indian Army, became fascinated, almost obsessed, with the mysterious ringings in his house.

He wrote a long letter to a local newspaper explaining what had occurred and asking for suggestions as to what had caused the phenomena. He got plenty of them; in addition, the newspaper received numerous accounts of similar incidents from its readers.

The bell ringing continued until the 27th of March when it stopped forever. No satisfactory explanation for the mysterious bells was ever offered.

Major Moor wrote a little book on his investigations. In it he declared:

"I will here, note, once and for all—that after much consideration, I cannot reach any procedure by which they [these effects] have been, or can be produced.

"If I had a year to devote to such considerations, and the promise of a thousand pounds in the event of discovery, I should despair of success. I would not, indeed, attempt it."

For those interested in psychical research the episode of the Bealings Bells has been regarded as sort of a classic poltergeist case. Major Moor was a member of the prestigious Royal Society, and the investigation that he conducted was very elaborate —but it was also very strange.

For example, in his book Major Moor gives a very detailed description of the arrangement of his bell system. But the description is so confusing that no one has ever been able to figure out how the bells were supposed to have worked. The confusion seems deliberate rather than the result of bad writing.

The most obvious explanation for the mysteriously ringing bells was that someone rang them deliberately. Major Moor made a detailed record of the temperature and barometric pressure during the period of the bell ringing, but he made no attempt to keep track of the people in his house.

One of the responses Major Moor got to his original letter in the newspaper came from a J. N. Maskelyne. Maskelyne suggested a very sensible plan of action. Enlist the aid of some trustworthy neighbors and friends. Then take everybody in the household and lock them in a room guarded over by a friend. Station other friends at various strategic points in the house, so that no one would be able to enter or leave undetected. Then search the house room by room, locking each room as the search continued.

"If this plan be pursued I will . . . make any moderate bet, either that the bells will not ring at all during the search, or that if they do ring, the party searching the house will find some relative or friend, or one of his establishment concealed in some part of the house."

Unfortunately Major Moor dismissed this excellent suggestion. ". . . I did not in any way, follow the advice therein offered."

What did the good Major conclude about the origin of his ghostly bells?

"The question ever recurs—what can be the cause? An adequate cause must exist; for these effects, and for every effect; moral and physical, in nature. But, in this case, no one has yet pretended so far as I know, to develop it.

"It may be no advance to say—that possibly, some hitherto undiscovered law of electricity or galvanism—latent—brought

53

into activity, only by certain combinations of metallic alloys, in certain concurring, or varied degrees of tension—in connection with certain conditions of atmospheric influences—acted upon by agencies, subtle and occult, &c. &c.

"These possibilities—whose combined eventualities may, or may not ever be developed—may be only another link in the amazing chain of results, that recent researchers into the mysterious operations of science and galvanics, have brought under the wondering eye and contemplation of chymical philosophy.

"Who can say, or imagine, where they are to end? . . ."

Does all that sound rather confusing? Of course it does. It's simply meaningless mumbo jumbo, perhaps deliberately meaningless at that. There is more than a suspicion that the whole episode of the Bealings Bells was a joke, not that someone was playing a joke on Major Moor, but that the Major was playing a joke on everyone else. His book may have been conceived as a gentle satire on investigations of other odd phenomena. If satire was his aim then he was a bit too gentle, for today the Bealings Bells is still frequently cited as one of the best poltergeist cases.

THE VERSAILLES ADVENTURE

Did you ever have the feeling that you had stepped into the past? I think we all have had feelings like that momentarily, when we see or hear something that reminds us of things that happened long ago. We know such a feeling is an illusion, nothing more. But if someone really believed that they had stepped into the past and walked among persons who had died a century or more ago, then we would have a proper ghost story. There is one incident in the annals of psychical research which fits this description.

The story began on the afternoon of August 10, 1901. Two Englishwomen, Anne Moberly and Eleanor Jourdain, who were touring in France, visited the great palace at Versailles outside of Paris. (When they later wrote up their experiences of that day they used the pseudonyms Elizabeth Morrison and Frances Lamont.) Both women were schoolteachers. They had no particular interest in French history in general or Versailles in particular. Nor had they any previous interest in psychical subjects or ghosts. They were quite ordinary tourists.

The pair was strolling toward the Petit Trianon, a smaller palace on the grounds of the main palace. The Petit Trianon had been a favorite spot of the unfortunate queen, Marie Antoinette. The two women saw a small gate, went through it, and their adventure began.

"To our right we saw some farm buildings looking empty and deserted; implements were lying about; we looked in, but saw no one. The impression was saddening; but it was not until we reached the crest of the rising ground where there was a garden that we began to feel as if we had lost our way, and as if something were wrong."

The two women found the atmosphere increasingly oppressive. The buildings and gardens around them looked somehow unreal, like they were all part of a stage set. They met two men who were wearing long greenish coats that looked like official uniforms of some sort. The men told them to go straight on. The feeling that something was very wrong became more and more overpowering. They passed a small round building which they called a kiosk. They saw a dark, pock-marked man wearing a wide brimmed hat and a heavy cloak. The expression on the man's face was "very evil," and they were almost afraid to walk past him.

The Petit Trianon at Versailles where two Englishwomen were supposed to have stepped into the past

They saw "a young girl standing in a doorway, who wore a white kerchief and dress to her ankles"; there was a lady sketching and finally they came to a country house. A young man offered to show them around to the front of the house and after he left them they stepped back into the twentieth century.

Oddly enough the two women did not talk about the incident for a full week. Wrote one, ". . . nor did I think about it until I began writing a descriptive letter of our expeditions of the week before. As the scenes came back one by one, the same sensations of dreamy unnatural oppression came over me so strongly that I stopped writing and said to Miss Lamont, 'Do you think that the Petit Trianon is haunted?' Her answer was prompt. 'Yes I do.' "

The women agreed not to talk about the incident any further, but to write out separate accounts of what they had experienced, and then compare them. The written accounts were similar enough to make the women believe that they had jointly experienced something very strange. They decided to do further research on Versailles.

Over the next two years the women spent hours searching books and memoirs concerning Versailles. They decided that they had stepped back into the past at a period shortly before the French Revolution overwhelmed King Louis XVI and Queen Marie Antoinette. From old maps and descriptions they believed that they were able to reconstruct exactly where they had walked that day. They thought that they could identify one of the individuals that they had seen. The dark-skinned, pock-marked man must have been the queen's Creole friend, the Comte de Vaudreuil, who was often at the palace. They believed that they were even able to fix the date upon which they had entered the past as August 5, 1789.

Three years after the first adventure, on July 4, 1904, the two women again visited Versailles. Nothing was the same. "The kiosk was gone. Instead of a shaded meadow continuing up to the wall of the terreace, there is now a broad gravel sweep beneath it. . . . Exactly where the lady was sitting, we found a large spreading bush of apparently many year's growth." The crowds in the modernized Trianon gardens in no way resembled the quaintly garbed individuals they had seen on their first visit. "The commonplace, unhistorical atmosphere was totally inconsistent with the air of silent mystery by which we had been so much oppressed. People went wherever they liked, and no one would think of interfering to show the way."

The two women finally wrote up their Versailles experience in a book called *An Adventure*. The case became, and remains, one of the most interesting and puzzling in the history of psychical research. The major reason this case has been taken so seriously is the very high caliber of the witnesses. There is, after all, no confirming evidence that Miss Moberly and Miss Jourdain saw what they said they saw. We just have to take their word for it. But everyone who has studied the case has assumed that their word was good. They were highly intelligent and very respectable individuals. They never sought money or fame from their experience. There has never been a hint that either of the women was a habitual liar or was in any way mentally unbalanced. The witnesses seemed just as puzzled about what they had experienced as everybody else was.

Well then, what did happen at Versailles on August 10, 1901? As usual we can't give any firm answers. A lot of people still believe that the two really did step back into the past. But a lot of people don't.

Many think that the whole incident was the result of wishful thinking and a vivid imagination. Says psychologist Joseph Jastrow, "One may suppose that the original impression is a vivid projection of the imagination prompted by a fleeting, unacknowledged flash-thought, which has flitted through thousands of tourists' minds. If articulate it would say: 'Wouldn't it be thrilling to see Versailles as it was in Marie Antoinette's day!' In this instance no sooner thought than seen."

In the 1930's an English psychical researcher named R. J. Sturge-Whiting carefully went over the whole case. By a diligent search he located all the places the women had described in their account, and concluded that they were all at Versailles in modern times. The people they had seen were gardeners, amateur artists, and ordinary tourists, the sort that visited the palace regularly. What about the identification of the Comte de Vaudreuil? Their description was very general. Surely there has been more than one dark, pock-marked man in history. It is not stretching coincidence too far to imagine that one was a tourist at Versailles on August 10, 1901.

It may seem astonishing that anyone could honestly misidentify the clothes. But it is important to remember that the clothes worn in 1901 were not as different from those worn in 1792, as today's clothes are from those worn in 1901. One writer has also pointed out that nowhere in their accounts do the women mention knee breeches, one of the most conspicuous features of men's clothing in 1792, but one which had disappeared long before 1901,

To set the whole mysterious and wonderful Versailles adventure down to a combination of a too active imagination and a case of mistaken identity seems rather disappointing. And perhaps it is not correct. Perhaps the two women did somehow step into the past. But the Versailles adventure certainly does not provide conclusive and indisputable proof that we can step into the past, or that the ghosts of the past can be momentarily resurrected, no matter how much we would like them to be.

THE GHOSTLY MONKS OF GLASTONBURY

There is perhaps no more mysterious place in England, indeed in all the world, than Glastonbury Abbey. Glastonbury Abbey is the site of one of the oldest, if not the oldest, Christian church in the British Isles. Long before it was a Christian church Glastonbury served as a pagan place of worship.

Legend has it that Christianity was first brought to Glastonbury by St. Joseph of Arimathea, the wealthy Jew who was supposed to have taken Jesus' body and placed it in the tomb he had prepared for himself. King Arthur is supposed to have

St. Michael's Chapel, atop Glastonbury Tor. The ancient Abbey at Glastonbury is surrounded with ghostly legends.

been buried at Glastonbury (and in fact, he may really have been buried there). The Holy Grail was taken to Glastonbury, according to some legends.

Naturally there are plenty of ghost stories attached to Glastonbury Abbey, including one which asserts that the ghost of King Arthur rides into the courtyard of the Abbey every Christmas Eve. But these are folk tales. However, there is one set of ghosts or spirits or what have you that deserves special attention.

Early in this century an antiquary and archaeologist named Frederick Bligh Bond and his colleague, J. Allan Bartlett, were appointed to take charge of the excavations at Glastonbury Abbey. Since the Abbey is very ancient, some sort of archaeological excavation is always going on there, even today.

Bond and Bartlett, however, were not ordinary archaeologists interested only in what they could see and measure. Both believed firmly in ghosts or spirits, or something very like them.

While at Glastonbury they decided to experiment with automatic writing. One of the men held a pencil in his hand, and the pair talked casually of indifferent matters. Then, sometimes the man holding the pencil would find his hand beginning to write. He was not supposed to guide the pencil himself. His hand was believed to be under the control of some sort of outside intelligence.

The first message came through on the night of November 7, 1907. It was supposed to have contained a floor plan of Glastonbury, and it was signed Gulielmus Monachus, William the Monk. Messages from other monks, who all indicated that they had lived at Glastonbury in about the thirteenth century, followed. The first messages were written in Latin, the language of medieval monks. But they soon switched to English, though it was a very archaic and strange kind of English. Often it was impossible to understand what the messages meant.

Cases of automatic writing are common enough. People who believe in communication with the dead find them very interesting and significant. But there is usually no way to prove that the person holding the pencil is actually being guided by some sort of outside force. However, if the messages produced by automatic writing contain information that could not possibly have been known by any living person, then that would be impressive.

The ghostly monks of Glastonbury began sending messages about the original construction of Glastonbury. They told the archaeologists what they would find when they dug. That was something no mortal man could know.

"When you dig, excavate the pillars of the crypt, six feet below the grass . . . they will give you a clue. The direction of the walls eastwards . . . was an angle . . . clothyards twenty seven long, nineteen wide. Wait and the course will open in the spring.

An automatic drawing of a chapel in Glastonbury Abbey. In the center of the drawing is the signature of the ghostly Gulielmus Monachus, William the Monk.

You will learn as you proceed. . . . We have much to do this season."

On the basis of such messages the two archaeologists claimed to have unearthed a chapel, the existence of which was unknown to any living person and not in any existing historical records.

A most satisfying ghost story so far. But as usual there is a catch. Other experts who examined both the messages and the results of the investigation were not at all impressed. Wrote one, "This automatic script, while it makes incorrect statements, disclosed nothing new which was true; and all might have been gathered from existing historical records or from careful observation and deduction."

If the two individuals who had produced the automatic script had been ordinary laymen then we might have to look at the case very differently. Even if the messages were vague and occasionally wrong, they were written in medieval Latin and archaic English, and contained a lot of architectural terms, as well as indicating an intimate knowledge of Glastonbury. However, since Bond and his associate were trained archaeologists and scholars, they had all of the necessary knowledge to produce the messages without any help from the dead.

The two men did not have to fake the messages deliberately. We must remember that both men were already strongly convinced that communication with the dead by automatic writing was possible. Today most people explain the messages by saying that the writers were guided by their own subconscious desires to communicate with the dead, and not by the spirit of a thirteenth-century monk.

THE GHOST AND THE JUDGE

There are hundreds of accounts of the ghost of a dying man appearing at some distant place, at the moment of his death. Usually these stories are very hard to check on. Therefore, striking as they seem at first glance, they do not provide conclusive proof for the existence of ghosts.

But there was one case of such an apparition that seemed so well attested to that it provided virtually irrefutable proof of the existence of ghosts. The witness in the case seemed utterly beyond reproach. He was Sir Edmund Hornby, who was at the time Chief Judge of the Supreme Consular Court of China and Japan at Shanghai.

It was the practice of the court to deliver judgments in the morning. But Sir Edmund would write out his judgments the night before, and give them to a local reporter so that they could appear in the paper on the morning that they were delivered.

On January 19, 1875, the judge wrote out his judgment an hour or two after dinner as usual. He then put it in an envelope and gave it to his butler, with instructions that the butler should give it to the reporter when he arrived. The judge then went to bed.

He was awakened by a knocking on his bedroom door. He said, "Come in," and to his surprise the reporter entered. "You have mistaken the door; but the butler has the judgment, so go and get it," the judge said. But the reporter did not leave and the judge began to get angry. The reporter, he noticed, "looked deadly pale, but was dressed as usual, and sober, and said, 'I know I am guilty of an unwarrantable intrusion, but finding that you were not in your study, I have ventured to come here.'"

By now the judge was having a very hard time controlling his temper. "But something in the man's manner disinclined me to jump out of bed and to eject him by force." Once again he ordered the reporter to leave the room; "Instead of doing so he put his hand on the foot-rail and gently, as if in pain, sat down on the foot of the bed. I glanced at the clock and saw that it was about twenty minutes past one.

"'Time presses,' said the reporter. 'Pray give me a précis of your judgment, and I will make a note in my book of it,' drawing his reporter's book out of his breast pocket. I said, 'I will do nothing of the kind. Go downstairs, find the butler, and don't disturb me—you will wake my wife; otherwise I shall have you put out.' He slightly moved his hand. I said, 'Who let you in?' He answered, 'No one.' 'Confound it,' I said, 'what the devil do you mean? Are you drunk?' He replied quickly, 'No, and never shall be again; but I pray your lordship give me your decision because time is short.' I said, 'You don't seem to care about my time, and this is the last time I will ever allow a reporter in my house.' He stopped me short by saying, 'This is the last time I shall ever see you anywhere.'"

The judge, still fearful that the commotion would awaken his wife in the next room, decided to give the reporter the summary he had asked for. The reporter took down what he was told, apparently in shorthand, thanked the judge and left. The clock was striking half past one.

The following day Judge Hornby learned that the reporter he had talked to had died suddenly that very night. The reporter had gone to his room to work. At about twelve o'clock his wife looked in to ask when he was coming to bed. He said, "I have only the judge's judgment to get ready, and then I have finished." When he had not come to bed by one-thirty she looked in on him again and found him on the floor dead. Alongside of him was his reporter's notebook.

The doctor estimated that the reporter had been dead since about one o'clock. The notebook contained these words, "In the Supreme Court, before the Chief Judge: The Chief Judge gave judgment this morning in the case to the following effect . . ." This was followed by a few lines of indecipherable shorthand.

Naturally enough, the judge inquired more fully into the circumstances of the reporter's death. At the inquest into the death the coroner decided that the reporter had died quite naturally of a heart attack. The reporter's wife and servants confirmed that he had not left the house on the night of his death. The judge's servants assured him that neither the reporter nor anyone else could have entered his house that night because all the doors and windows had been locked.

The judge had no desire to make his "spiritual experience," as he called it, public. So he told only a few close friends. He also asked his wife to confirm what she could remember of that night. She did seem to recall hearing her husband talking to someone during the night, but she did not hear what they had said.

Nine years after the event, when psychical researchers Edmund Gurney and Frederic Myers approached Sir Edmund, he decided to make the whole story public, and dictated the account which is quoted here.

The judge was very sure that his account was accurate. "As I said then, so I say now—I was not asleep, but wide awake. After a lapse of nine years my memory is quite clear on the subject. I have not the least doubt I saw the man—I have not the least doubt that the conversation took place between us."

A perfect ghost story—and it was all true. At least so it seemed for several months after Gurney and Myers published the details of the case. Then a letter arrived from a Mr. Frederick H. Balfour who pointed out certain vital discrepancies between the judge's story and the facts of the case.

1. The reporter whose name was the Reverend Hugh Lang Nivens, editor of the *Shanghai Courier,* had not died at one in the morning. Rather he died between 8 and 9 A.M. after having a good night's rest.

2. The judge was not married at the time of Reverend Nivens' death. His second wife had died two years previously and he did not remarry until three months after the death of Reverend Nivens.

3. No inquest was ever held in the case.

4. "The story turns upon the judgment of a certain case to be delivered the next day, January 20, 1875. There is no record of any such judgment."

When the judge saw Balfour's letter he was astonished, but he did not really disagree with it.

"My vision must have followed the death [by some three months] instead of synchronizing with it," he wrote. "At the same time this hypothesis is quite contrary to the recollection of the facts in both my own mind and in Lady Hornby's mind. . . . If I had not believed, as I still believe, every word of it [the story] was accurate, and that my memory was to be relied on, I should not ever have told it as a personal experience."

It seems fairly obvious that the judge was an honest man. He had nothing to gain and quite a bit of reputation to lose by lying. Could he have been so grossly mistaken? As a jurist he should have been trained in the observation of detail and in weighing evidence. But nine years passed between the time of the experience and the time it was written down. Memory can play strange tricks in that period of time.

Perhaps the fault lies with Balfour. Did he get his facts wrong, or did he for some unknown reason deliberately distort the facts in order to tarnish the judge's story?

The case is hopelessly confused.

There you have a selection of some of the best *real* ghost stories, from medieval times to the early years of this century. As spooky and interesting as many of them are, it is quite obvious that conclusive proof for the existence of ghosts is going to be hard to come by.

These ghost stories are what psychical researchers call "spontaneous" experiences. They may happen at any time—there is no predicting when and where. Such events are hard to study closely. In order to prove the existence of ghosts or spirits, the researchers had to find a more regular way of establishing contact with them.

With the development of a movement called spiritualism, this regular contact with the dead seemed to be established.

3

The Spirits Speak

You might get the impression that ghosts prefer the castles, stately homes, and ancient abbeys of Europe, particularly England. And, in fact, English ghosts are very famous. But probably the most influential ghost in all history appeared in the United States, and in humble surroundings.

This very important ghostly event took place in the little hamlet of Hydesville in upstate New York, about thirty miles east of the city of Rochester. There a series of strange happenings began in March of 1848. At that time Hydesville was a small but moderately prosperous farming community consisting of about forty houses. One of the poorer homes in town, a little ramshackle frame house, was occupied by the family of a farmer and part-time blacksmith named John D. Fox. The Fox family had only lived in the Hydesville house a few months. Before that the house had been occupied by a long succession of tenants. Mostly it had been used as a temporary dwelling by families looking for larger and more suitable quarters in the vicinity. The house had a reputation for being shabby and uncomfortable, but it had no reputation for being haunted.

Four members of the Fox family lived in the little house.

The house of the Fox family in Hydesville, where the "spirit" rappings were first heard.

Mr. Fox was a morose and silent man, and a staunch Methodist. People said that before he had turned to religion he had been a drunkard for many years. His religion, however, had not improved his disposition. Mrs. Fox was known as a good woman, who had endured a hard life during her husband's drinking years. She was not considered terribly bright.

With the couple lived two young daughters, Margaretta, sometimes called Margaret or Maggie, who was fifteen years old and Kate (also called Katie, Cathie, or Catharine) who was not quite twelve. There were two other Fox children, much older than Maggie and Kate, who no longer lived with their parents. A son David lived a few miles from Hydesville. A married daughter, thirty-four years old, Leah Fish, lived in Rochester. Leah was separated from her husband at the time, and ultimately ran through several husbands.

During the last week of March, 1848, the Fox household was

shaken by a series of strange noises, for which no cause could be found. Most of the noises seemed to come from the room in which Maggie and Kate slept. The family was at first disturbed, then frightened. But after they decided that whatever was making the noises meant them no harm, they became curious. One night while in a rather playful mood, the girls began asking the mysterious noisemaker some questions. To everyone's apparent surprise the girls received understandable answers. When they asked "it" the age of one of the girls the correct number of knocks were given. This so astonished Mr. and Mrs. Fox that they invited the neighbors in to see, or rather to hear, what was going on.

One of the neighbors, William Duesler, wrote the following account of what he witnessed:

"Mrs Fox then asked if it would answer my questions if I asked any, and if so, rap. It then rapped three times. (This was the signal for yes.) I then asked if it was an injured spirit, and it rapped. I asked if it had come to hurt anyone who was present, and it did not rap. I then reversed the question, and it rapped. I asked if I or my father had injured it (as we had formerly lived in the house), and there was no noise. Upon asking the negative of these questions the rapping was heard. I then asked if Mr.—— [John C. Bell] (naming a person who had formerly lived in the house) had injured it, and if so, manifest it by rapping, and it made three knocks louder than common, and at the same time the bedstead jarred more than it had done before. I then inquired if it was murdered for money, and the knocking was heard. I then requested it to rap when I mentioned the sum of money for which it was murdered. I then asked it if it was one hundred, two, three, or four, and when I came to five hundred the rapping was heard. All in the room said they heard it distinctly."

As the word of the Hydesville rappings spread, hundreds came to see the Fox house and to witness the marvel. They came on foot, on horseback, by wagon and coach. The little town had never seen such excitement before.

The rapping spirit indicated that its body had been buried in the cellar. The Foxes dug up the cellar, and according to one account they found some human teeth and bones and parts of a broken bowl. But this story, like so much about the Hydesville rappings, has been disputed.

Now it happened that John C. Bell, the ghost's accused murderer, was living in a town not a dozen miles from Hydesville. He rushed back to confront his accuser face to face. But since his accuser was an invisible ghost, who had no face, this proved to be impossible. Instead, Bell went to his friends and former neighbors and asked them all to sign statements testifying to their belief in his innocence, and to his good character and reputation. Some forty-four persons signed such a statement, and Bell had it printed up and distributed in pamphlet form.

However, there was at least one person in Hydesville who did not care for John C. Bell at all. She was Lucretia Pulver, who had worked as a maid for the Bell family when they lived in Hydesville in 1844. Lucretia had been fourteen years old at the time. She said that she remembered seeing a peddler who had come to the house during the summer of 1884 and had promised to return. But the peddler had never been seen again. According to Lucretia, on the day after the peddler's disappearance she had been sent away from the house. She claimed that a few days later she saw Mrs. Bell mending two old overcoats, which she hinted might have belonged to the murdered peddler. She also mentioned seeing some loose earth in the cellar. The murdered man's grave perhaps? A couple of other people, including Lucretia's

The Fox family hears the first of the "spirit" rappings.

mother, added their belief that something unusual, and perhaps terrible, had happened in the house during the summer of 1844.

The rapping ghost who was so garrulous about most things turned surprisingly coy when it came to giving information about himself. The sisters, for no good reason, nicknamed him Mr. Splitfoot. He indicated that his initials were C. R. and that he had once lived in Orleans County, New York, and that he had five children. Attempts to confirm these meager leads came to nothing. Clearly, John C. Bell could not be charged with murder on the basis of such evidence. The authorities dismissed the whole affair as the creation of a group of mischievous girls.

So far, the Hydesville rappings looked like nothing more than a American version of the Cock Lane ghost. (It would be interesting to know if any of the Fox family had ever heard of the Cock Lane ghost before the rappings began. There is no evidence on this point one way or another.) Interest in the Cock Lane ghost ran high for a while, but it petered out quickly. Interest in the Hydesville rappings, and in the Fox sisters themselves, continued to grow.

The rappings provided the spark that set off a worldwide movement that came to be called spiritualism. Millions of people became involved in the spiritualist movement. Today spiritualism is not as popular as it once was, but it has by no means disappeared. Thus, the echoes of the Hydesville rappings can be heard in the 1970's.

How could it happen? How could such a simple, and really unspectacular, event create such a reaction? The fact is that a lot of people were ready for spiritualism in 1848. Anything might have set them off. The Hydesville rappings occurred at just the right moment, in the right place, and they got the right sort of publicity.

While a lot of people had begun to doubt the existence of ghosts altogether, many others began to look for ways to break down the barriers between the world of the living and the world of the dead. In the mid-nineteenth century the old religious taboos regarding talking to the spirits of the dead no longer were taken very seriously. Science had brought the whole idea of life after death into question, and a lot of people wanted to prove scientifically that man did survive death. Faith was not enough—what they wanted was evidence. Thus anything that seemed to offer tangible evidence of the existence of spirits was bound to be greeted with enormous interest and enthusiasm.

In 1744 a distinguished Swedish scientist named Emanuel Swedenborg announced that he could go into a trance and talk to the spirit of any dead person he chose. Swedenborg advised others not to try the procedure because they might be misled

73

by evil spirits. Swedenborg wrote dozens of long dull books, on the subject of the spirit world. Hardly anyone was able to read his books, but his ideas were still very influential.

At the end of the eighteenth and beginning of the nineteenth centuries the early hypnotists—mesmerists or magnetists as they were called at that time—were busily putting people into trances. At least some of these entranced individuals began reporting that they could talk to the spirits of the dead.

Hypnotism was slow to come to the United States, but by the mid-nineteenth century it had become popular. Hypnotists traveled from town to town giving lectures and demonstrations. Life in many of the towns and cities of early nineteenth-century America was pretty dull. The visit of a traveling hypnotist might be the most exciting event of the year. As soon as the hypnotist left, the people of the town would begin practicing what they had seen, on one another. One resident of Poughkeepsie, New York, bitterly complained that after the visit of a hypnotist in 1843, "almost everybody began mesmerizing each other."

One of the citizens of Poughkeepsie who proved to be an exceptionally good subject for hypnosis was an eighteen-year-old shoemaker's assistant named Andrew Jackson Davis. Davis would go into a trance and diagnose people's illnesses. He was considered so good at this that he left his job with the shoemaker, and became a professional hypnotic subject. He was supported by a wealthy tailor whose hobby was hypnosis.

Usually Davis awoke from a trance feeling refreshed, but one evening after being hypnotized he went to bed feeling very confused, and ill. He woke up in the middle of the night and, driven by some unknown compulsion, got dressed and wandered out into the fields, though it was the dead of winter. While sitting on a hill overlooking the Hudson River, Davis believed that he saw

74

the spirit of an ancient Greek physician Galen and the spirit of
before the Hydesville rappings began. Poughkeepsie, Davis'
he had a mission to elevate the human soul.

A short time later Davis, with the help of a few friends, began
to write a book. Davis never claimed to have actually "written"
the book himself. He said that he had merely acted as a trans-
mitter for invisible spirits who controlled him while he was in a
trance. He would go into a trance and begin dictating. His friends
would take down what he said.

The dictation was continued over a period of fourteen months,
and the resulting book, called *The Divine Revelations*, was published in 1847. It was an immediate and enormous success. It
wasn't so much what the book said that made it so popular. *The
Divine Revelations* was a long book filled with vague and wordy
pronouncements about the nature of man and of the universe. It
is hard to imagine that all of the people who bought the book
had even bothered to read it. What really caught the public fancy
was that this was supposed to be a book not written by any human hand, but rather one which had come directly from the spirit
world.

Andrew Jackson Davis' book was published less than a year
before the Hydesville rappings began. Poughkeepsie, Davis'
hometown, was all the way across New York State from Hydesville, but Davis' fame surely reached that far.

Therefore, even before the Hydesville rappings began the
people of upstate New York were already very interested in communicating with the spirit world. So it isn't really so surprising
that the noises heard in the Fox home set off such a great wave
of enthusiasm.

The loud rappings, as well as the crowds, began to bother the
Fox family. They decided that in the interest of peace and quiet

the girls should be sent away for a time. First Maggie and Kate went to the home of their brother David. But the rappings followed them and so did the hordes of curiosity seekers. The girls were then split up. Kate remained at her brother's house while Maggie was sent to Rochester to stay with her sister Leah.

In Rochester the rappings grew, if possible, worse than ever. They were accompanied, according to Leah, by a host of other activities typical of a poltergeist. Objects were thrown about, beds were shaken, and tables and chairs moved mysteriously about the rooms. Along with the raps there were mysterious shouts, groans, grunts, and a sound that Leah described as the gurgle of coagulated blood being emptied from a bucket.

But rather than being mindless and destructive, as most poltergeists are supposed to be, this one remained generally cheerful and remarkably cooperative. It even helped some friends of the Foxes work out a rapping code by which more complex messages could be spelled out. The spirit was no longer limited to simple yes and no answers to questions. The first message delivered by this code was, "We are all your dear friends and relatives."

The significance of the rappings seems to have expanded dramatically. No longer was the source of the noises simply the spirit of a murdered peddler intent upon bringing his murderer to justice. The rappings now appeared to open up a channel of communication to the world of the dead. It was a "spiritual telegraph" as its supporters called it. The word "telegraph" was popular at this time because four years earlier Samuel Morse had made his first succesful experiments with the telegraph. The world was still astonished by the apparent miracles of sending coded messages over a wire. The rappings of the spirits and the tapping of the telegraph machine sounded very much alike. To many the spiritual telegraph seemed no more incomprehensible or miraculous than Samuel Morse's telegraphy, though considerably more wonderful, and more important.

The gift of stimulating messages from the spirit world proved to be contagious. Soon the rappings began to follow Leah, as well as her younger sisters. When one of the Fox girls stayed in a boarding house other girls in the house quite suddenly developed the ability to produce rappings.

A person through whom the spirits are supposed to speak, whether by rapping or by any other means, is called a medium. While the Fox sisters were not actually supposed to make the noises themselves, the spirits could only produce raps or other manifestations while a medium was present. Mediums were, in a sense, like the wires of Mr. Morse's telegraph. Within two years after the Hydesville rappings began there were hundreds of professional and nonprofessional mediums in the United States, and the practice was spreading to Europe. Like the Fox sisters, most mediums—though certainly not all—were women.

This belief that the living could communicate with the dead through the agency of a medium was dubbed spiritualism. A mere six years after the rappings were first heard in the Fox house, some 15,000 American spiritualists gathered together for a convention. They were angry that the government did not seem to have paid proper attention to their movement. They sent a petition to Congress requesting official recognition. However, the congressmen refused to take their petition seriously. One senator suggested that the petition be referred to the Committee on Foreign Relations: "We may have occasion to enter into diplomatic relations with the spirits." Another congressman suggested, for some unknown reason, that the petition be sent to the Committee on Military Affairs. The congressmen had a good laugh over the

The Fox sisters, Margaretta, Catharine, and Leah

whole thing, and promptly forgot about the petition. But the spiritualists had not been joking. They were in dead earnest about what they believed.

While many mediumistic stars appeared during the early years of spiritualism the Fox sisters remained among the most famous.

The sisters may first have been shy about the rappings that seemed to follow them about, but they soon lost all traces of shyness. From private performances, or sittings, as they came to be called, the Fox sisters moved onto the public stage. In conjunction with a local hypnotist, Dr. George Capron, Leah and Maggie participated in a series of lectures and demonstrations in Rochester. A crowd of four hundred attended the first night of the series. Unfortunately, in the crowd was a group of jokesters with firecrackers. They broke up the demonstration. The following nights were more successful. The Fox sisters moved from town to town in upstate New York, attracting large crowds wherever they went. By 1850 they felt secure enough to take their demonstrations to New York City itself, and they were an enormous success.

Naturally, not everyone believed that the spirits were responsible for the noises. Many people believed that the Fox sisters faked the noises, somehow. But for every prominent scoffer there was an equally prominent supporter. Many skeptical people went to meet the Fox sisters and were deeply impressed. One of those who was quickly converted to the new cause of spiritualism was Horace Greeley, the editor of the *New York Tribune,* and one of the most important figures in the history of American journalism. Wrote Greeley in August of 1850:

"Mrs. Fox and her three daughters left our city yesterday on their return to Rochester, after a stay of some weeks, during which they have freely subjected the mysterious influence by which they seem to be accompanied to every reasonable test, and to the keen and critical scrutiny of the hundreds who have chosen to visit them, or whom they have been invited to visit. . ."

Shortly after word of the Hydesville rappings spread, Andrew Jackson Davis visited the Fox sisters. He came away convinced of the genuineness of the phenomena. Davis was highly respected among those who were inclined to believe in spiritualism, so his endorsement counted for a great deal.

The rappings that accompanied the Fox sisters seemed to provide what the spirits had otherwise lacked—tangible, scientific proof of their existence. Now, admittedly, rapping noises aren't very impressive when compared to the headless ghosts or other awful apparitions of fiction. They even seemed rather tame when compared to benign apparitions, like those reported by trustworthy witnesses from time to time. But the rappings had one great advantage; they were reasonably reliable. No one could ever be guaranteed of seeing a ghost at any particular time. Ghosts stubbornly refused to appear at the stroke of midnight in even the best haunted houses. But if a witness went to one of the Fox sisters' demonstrations, he could be guaranteed of at least hearing noises that were supposed to be produced by spirits of the dead.

The spirits that followed the Fox sisters could be tested in two ways. In the first place, the sisters themselves could be tested to see if they were producing the noise by some secret, but perfectly normal, means—in other words, faking. Secondly, the ghosts could be questioned to see if they could provide answers that were not, or should not have been, known to the medium. The Fox sisters' spirits seemed to succeed at both tests.

In the early days of spiritualism most of the tests concentrated on finding out whether the Fox sisters themselves produced the knockings. A lot of people quite naturally suspected that they were faking the noises, but for several years no one was able to put forth a convincing explanation of how the faking was done, though the girls were repeatedly observed, searched, and tested.

Then, early in the year 1851, the Fox sisters went to Buffalo, New York. There they were seen by three doctors from the University of Buffalo. The doctors believed that the noises the sisters attributed to the spirits were actually produced by movements of their knee joints.

Practically all of us can crack our knuckles, that is, make snapping sounds by stretching or bending our knuckles. Sometimes the snapping can be very loud, particularly if a person has practiced doing it. Perhaps you have had the experience of having your knee, or elbow, or even your back "crack." You may have straightened up suddenly and heard a loud cracking sound, and perhaps felt a slight pain. The sound can be so loud that your first thought might have been that you had somehow broken a bone. But, in fact, only a slight involuntary movement of the tendons of the joint caused the noise.

The three Buffalo doctors believed that the Fox sisters had perfected the art of cracking the joints of their knees very loudly to make the "spirit" rappings. They said they knew a lady who could produce sounds just like those made by the Fox sisters' "spirit" by snapping her knee joints.

The doctors published their theory in the form of a letter in a Buffalo newspaper. Leah was enraged by the charge and challenged the doctors to prove the truth of their accusation. So a test was arranged.

At first there were plenty of raps for the doctors to hear. But then the doctors seated the Fox sisters on cushions and arranged their legs in such a way that they believed that snapping of the knee joints would be impossible. According to the doctor's report, "The company, seated in a semicircle, quietly waited for the 'manifestations' for more than half an hour, but the 'spirits,' generally so noisy, were now dumb. . . On resuming the usual position on the sofa, the feet resting on the floor, knockings very soon began to be heard."

A further test was tried. The doctors grasped the girls' knees. For most of the time, while the girls' knees were being held, there were no knockings, though there were plenty of them when their knees were not being held. There were two or three faint knocks while the doctors were holding the sisters' knees, and one doctor said that he distinctly felt the joints of one knee move.

81

Worse was yet to come for the Fox sisters. Just a few weeks after the Buffalo doctors published their findings, a Mrs. Norma Culver, a relative of the Fox sisters, said that the sisters had confessed to her how the rappings were made—mostly by snapping their knees and toe joints. They had also explained to her many of the other tricks of their trade, such as how to watch the face of a person asking a question, so they could know whether the "spirits" were giving the correct answer.

"Catharine [Kate] told me how to manage to answer the questions. She said it was generally easy enough to answer right if the one who asked the questions called the alphabet [in order to get the 'spirit' to rap yes to the correct letter]. She said the reason why they asked people to write down several names on paper, and then point to them till the spirit rapped at the right one, was to give them a chance to watch the countenance and motions of the person, and in that way they could nearly always guess right."

This was damning indeed, for Mrs. Culver added that she had on several occasions actually helped the girls produce their illusions, and that she had mastered the art of joint snapping herself.

The Fox sisters flatly denied all of these charges. They pointed out some factual errors in Mrs. Culver's statement, and claimed that the whole thing was a lie inspired by family jealousy. Many of those who had seen the Fox sisters and been impressed by their demonstrations simply could not believe that the loud rappings they had heard had been produced by anything as ordinary as the snapping of toe or knee joints. The testimony of the Buffalo doctors and Mrs. Culver's accusation may have created some doubts, but they did not slow the growth of spiritualism, and they hardly damaged the Fox sisters' reputation.

However, as the influence of spiritualism increased, so its opponents gathered more evidence against it. A man named Chauncy Burr, a fierce opponent of spiritualism, perfected the joint snapping trick and toured the East giving lectures against spiritualism. He concluded his lectures by loudly snapping his toe joints.

A number of mediums who tried to cash in on the success of the Fox sisters confessed that they had produced spirit knocks by trickery. The most sensational confession was that of thirteen-year-old Almira Bezely which came in October, 1851. The girl had been a medium for several months, and during one of her sittings the "spirits" predicted the death of her baby brother. Almira then proceeded to murder the child. She was tried and convicted of the crime. During her trial she explained how she had produced the rappings with her feet.

However, confirmed spiritualists were not badly shaken by such revelations either. Of course, they agreed, there were false mediums, but there were genuine mediums as well. If one, or a dozen, or a hundred mediums were shown to be tricksters, they reasoned, this did not prove that *all* mediums were. Spiritualists came to believe that even some genuine mediums were occasionally forced to fake their "manifestations." Sometimes, said the supporters of spiritualism, the spirits were not particularly cooperative. In order not to disappoint her followers or damage her own reputation, the medium might then be tempted to resort to trickery. If a medium was caught using trickery this did not automatically prove that she used it all the time.

Even when a medium confessed to using trickery all of the time this was not considered conclusive by those who believed strongly in spiritualism. Over the years spiritualists had come to the rather sad conclusion that mediums, though they possessed special powers, were strange and often unreliable individuals. They might make false confessions of trickery out of sheer malice. Or they might do it because they needed money and thought they could make some from a false "exposé." The anti-spiritualists might also somehow force a medium into making a false confession.

Such beliefs about the confessions of mediums were widely held by spiritualists. Thus, when the Fox sisters themselves—who were really responsible for starting spiritualism in the first place—confessed that they had been faking all along, the spiritualists were not particularly upset.

The confession of the Fox sisters came in the year 1888, some thirty years after the first rappings in Hydesville. First Margaret and then Catharine Fox made public statements that the rappings had been fraudulent from the very beginning and that all spiritualism was a fraud. They explained how the noises had been made. Margaret even gave demonstrations before large audiences showing how the noises had been made.

According to the sisters the rappings first began as a sort of childish joke to frighten their mother. The first raps had been produced by dropping apples on the floor. But soon the girls learned how to snap their joints, and this became the principle method of producing "spirit" noises. Gloated one antispiritualist newspaper, Margaret Fox has "located the origin of spiritualism in her great toe."

In the beginning, said Margaret, she and her sister had been flattered and pleased by all the attention they received because of the rappings. But neither of the younger Fox sisters had any particular plan to make money or become famous. The real force behind the success of the Fox sisters was their older sister, Leah. Leah was never particularly good at snapping her joints, but she was very good at managing her sisters. Margaret wrote, "In Rochester [our sister] gave exhibitions. We had crowds coming to see us and she made as much as $100 to $150 a night. . . Katie and I were led around like lambs. We drew immense crowds. . ."

There is something very sad about the Fox sisters' confession. By 1888 spiritualism had grown far beyond their wildest dreams. They had never been able to control the movement they started, or even to understand it, and they had long been eclipsed by more spectacular and clever mediums. The sisters, despite their former fame, were paupers by the time they made their confessions, and both were hopeless alcoholics. Ultimately, at least Margaret recanted her confession, saying that she made a false confession because she needed the money. The spiritualists welcomed her back into the fold.

That is how modern spiritualism began. Even today among those interested in psychic phenomena the Fox sisters are the subject of controversy. Practically everyone is willing to admit that the sisters faked at least some of the rappings. But many do not believe that they were all faked. The "exposures" of the Fox sisters, they say, came from persons who had strong prejudices against them in the first place.

Nor do supporters of the Fox sisters think much of the confessions produced when the women were shattered and poverty stricken. They tend rather to accept Margaret's recantation.

Supporters of the sisters insist that not all of the rappings attributed to them could possibly have been produced by joint snapping. Even antispiritualists agree with this. They believe that the sisters used a variety of techniques under different conditions. They claim that the sisters often used hidden accomplices who would rap on signal. The antispiritualists point out that professional magicians generally have several different ways of producing a single effect.

If the Fox sisters were all that there ever was to spiritualism then we would have to set the case aside as an oddity of history. But the sisters, as we have seen, were only the starting point, and a very modest starting point at that.

4

Secrets of the Séance

The Fox sisters' spirit peddler first merely rapped out simple answers to simple questions. The spirits then moved on to tapping out short messages in code. But once the initial excitement wears off, such a "spiritual telegraph" can become pretty tedious. It might take hours to rap out even a short message. Before long the phenomena produced by the spiritualists went far beyond this primitive stage.

Let us try to imagine what it was like to attend a spiritualist séance in the late nineteenth century. A séance is defined as a meeting or gathering held for the purpose of communicating with the dead.

There were both professional and nonprofessional mediums. The professionals made their living as mediums, and traveled from place to place. The nonprofessionals were more numerous but they usually exercised their talents only within a group of family or friends.

Since the professional mediums generally held more spectacular séances, let us imagine that you are attending a séance with a famous professional medium. In this case the séance is being held at the medium's home. While on tour the medium might

87

hold séances in the homes of wealthy spiritualist friends or in hotel rooms. There were also mediums who would hold large public séances or demonstrations in auditoriums or halls. But the whole mood of such performances was vastly different from the mood created at a private séance. Many convinced spiritualists tended to distrust those mediums who performed in public. There was a strong suspicion that such persons were just showmen, rather than true mediums.

One could not simply drop in on a private séance being held in a private home. Such meetings were not advertised, and were open by invitation only. You were invited to this séance by a good friend who was already deeply interested in spiritualism, and knew the medium personally. There was no admission fee, but as in any church service, offerings were gratefully accepted. Sitters were usually generous.

When you arrive, there are already ten people at the home of the medium waiting to participate in the séance. With you and your friend there will be an even dozen—a fairly typical number for a séance. You are the only "first timer" in the group. All of the others have attended at least one other séance, and several members of the group have been regular sitters with this medium for months or years. To one degree or another, everyone aside from yourself is already committed to believing in the truth of spiritualism. Disbelievers, particularly those who noisily voice their opinions, are not invited back for a second séance. You are told that just a few weeks ago, someone had mistakenly invited a loud-mouthed skeptic. This fellow implied that the medium was a fraud and he raised such a fuss that the spirits would not appear that evening and the whole séance was called off. It was great disappointment. No one wanted to see the same mistake made again.

The séance is to be held in a spacious, comfortable room. You all seat yourselves around a large circular table. The medium suggests that in order to get in the right mood a little singing might be in order. One of the sitters goes to the piano and begins to play some familiar hymns. The group joins in singing enthusiastically, and expectation builds. After a few hymns the medium announces that she is ready.

Now the séance proper is about to begin. The gaslights are turned down, and a screen is set in front of the fire, so that the room becomes very dark. You cannot make out the features of the person seated next to you, and you cannot see the medium at all. You have been told that the darkness is necessary, for the spirits do not like bright lights.

You are instructed to place your hands flat on the table, with your thumbs touching one another. The little fingers of each hand are touching the little fingers of the persons sitting on each side of you. After what seems like an interminable period of absolute silence, a number of astonishing things begin to happen.

First you hear strange noises, knocks, and raps coming from various parts of the room. Then the table upon which you and the other sitters have your hands begins to rise and rock back and forth. It rocks with such force that you have to struggle to keep your hands on top of it, and you press down very hard because the table feels as though it is going to fly away.

Above your head and behind your back various musical instruments—tambourines, horns, and guitars—begin to play mysteriously. A cold breeze suddenly chills you, though before you sat down you were quite sure that all the windows and doors were securely closed. The air now smells perfumed. Something drops into your lap, and the shock startles you into jumping up, and you almost scream. (Later, after the lights are turned on

Table weighing forty-five pounds supposedly being levitated during a séance. The medium, Jack Webber, is tied to his chair. The photograph was taken during a séance by infrared light.

again, you discover what was dropped into your lap was only a bunch of flowers. Such objects, usually flowers or jewelry, which appear in the séance room, apparently from nowhere, are called "apports.")

After taking your seat again, and recovering a bit from the shock of having something dropped into your lap, you feel something else strange. It feels like someone is tugging at your garments under the table. Near where the medium is sitting you see a glowing object peek up over the edge of the table. It is a luminescent hand, but a tiny one like a child's hand. Abruptly the hand is pulled back and everything is in darkness again.

Then you hear the medium say, "I feel as if I am going to rise. Yes, yes, I am ascending." Someone else shouts, "She is. She is. Her shoe has just brushed my cheek." The medium cautions, "Please don't touch me or I shall fall."

The medium's voice seems to come from higher and higher, and when she says, "I am floating near the ceiling," her voice does come from near the ceiling. A faint glow is coming through the window, from a full moon outside. For a moment you catch a glimpse of the medium's feet and legs passing horizontally in front of the window. They are far off the ground.

A short time later the medium says, "I feel as if I am coming down." You hear the noises of a chair being pushed back. And one of the other sitters tells you that the medium has resumed her seat.

Near where the medium is seated a faint glowing patch appears in the air. It grows brighter, and seems to form into the likeness of a human face floating in the air. The face appears rigid and masklike. It seems to be covered by a luminous gauzy substance. The features are hardly discernible, yet one of the other sitters appears to recognize it as the face of a relative who has recently died. The glowing face hovers in the air for a few seconds, or for a few moments. In the darkness it is impossible to judge accurately the passage of time. Then it disappears.

Luminous clouds now appear in one corner of the room, near where you remember a large cabinet is standing. Abruptly the doors to the cabinet are thrown open and a ghostly female figure, draped in what appears to be luminescent gauze, steps out. Since the luminescent material covers the figure's face it is impossible to make out her features very closely. (Later you are informed that the figure was that of Katie King, the famous spirit control.)

91

The figure walks around the table silently, and touches all of the sitters lightly with her hand. The touch is solid enough, but feels unnaturally cold. Then she returns to the cabinet, the doors close, and all is in darkness once again.

After a short time you hear the medium groan and then say, "I think that is all for this evening, ladies and gentlemen." Someone turns the gaslights up again and you see everyone seated as they had been before the lights were turned out. The medium looks very tired, and asks what had taken place. She says she remembers nothing since she was in a trance for the entire séance. Everyone agrees that the séance had been a particularly successful one.

The séance just described is, of course, completely imaginary. But the various manifestations, the table tipping, the levitation, the materialization of spirit hands and heads are not. Such manifestations took place at thousands, perhaps hundreds of thousands, of séances during the last part of the nineteenth and early part of the twentieth century. Few séances were quite as eventful as the one described. Such manifestations as the levitation of the medium or the materialization of an entire spirit body were relatively rare—but they were reported—and lots of people believed in them.

The events described in the imaginary séance by no means exhaust all the possible manifestations that might take place at a spiritualist séance. Brief messages might appear mysteriously on blank slates; the medium might walk over to the fire and take out hot coals with her bare hands, or she might "grow" or "elongate" several inches during the course of a séance. On other

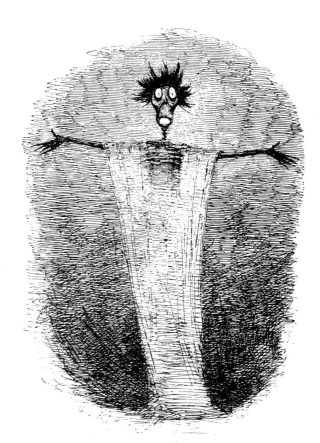

A nineteenth-century wood engraving of a skeleton-like ghost

occasions, when there was no complete materialization of a spirit, clouds or bands of a glowing material called *ectoplasm* seemed to eminate from the medium's head. The spirits might also speak, customarily through a trumpet that floated in the air. At a spiritualist séance practically anything might happen.

All of these various events were called "the physical phenomena," and the mediums who produced them were called physical mediums. Much of what they produced looked—to nonspiritualists at least—suspiciously like stage magic. Physical mediums were often accused of being conjurers or sleight-of-hand artists. In order to ward off such charges many mediums offered to hold séances while tied to their chairs or while inside of a sealed bag, or being held down by two witnesses or under any of a variety of other restraints.

Two of the most celebrated mediums of the early era of spiritualism, the Davenport brothers from Buffalo, New York, did not even bother to hold séances. They produced their phenomena on music hall stages throughout America and Europe. The brothers' main prop was a huge double-doored cabinet. One was seated in each side of the cabinet, and they were either tied or chained to their chairs. Yet they managed to make bells ring, and horns blow, and produce a large number of other startling phenomena.

As a matter of fact, the Davenport brothers never exactly claimed that the spirits were responsible for all the marvelous and mysterious things that took place at their demonstrations, but this is what most people believed, and the Davenports certainly made no effort at all to deny the power of the spirits.

Fakers or not, the Davenport brothers carried physical mediumship to its logical extreme. But there was another type of medium, one who did not deal with glowing figures or floating

MUSIC HALL.

THIS EVENING,

**AND EVERY EVENING DURING THE WEEK EXCEPT WEDNESDAY,
ALSO ON WEDNESDAY AND SATURDAY AFTERNOONS,**

THE WORLD-RENOWNED

DAVENPORT BROTHERS

Will appear after a most extraordinary and successful tour of four
years in Europe, in their unique and startling wonders, mysterious displays, and unaccountable manifestations.

*Poster advertising a performance by the Davenport Brothers who were
supposed to work wonders with the aid of "spiritual power."*

trumpets. This was the mental or "psychic" medium. Séances
with these mediums were not nearly as spectacular as were séances with the physical mediums. In the early days of spiritualism mental mediums were not nearly as popular as physical
mediums. But ultimately, as many of the physical mediums were
exposed as tricksters, or confessed to using sleight-of-hand to

95

produce their effects, the mental mediums came to dominate the field.

A séance with a mental medium began in pretty much the same way as a séance with a physical medium. A major difference was that the lights might be lowered, but not turned off. Mental mediums generally preferred to work in subdued light but not total darkness. The séance would begin with the medium going into a trance. Some mediums slipped into a trance quite easily and naturally. They merely slumped forward, as though they had fallen asleep. For others the onset of a trance might be quite violent. The medium might scream, become rigid, fall out of her chair, or actually go into convulsions. Such a display could be as frightening to the sitters at a séance as the appearance of any ghostly figure might be.

Once in a trance, the medium would begin to speak, but in a voice very different from her normal voice. At this point the medium was supposed to be under the influence of a spirit "control." The control was another link in the chain between this world and the next. Controls, it seemed, were those spirits especially chosen to contact the living. They were, in a sense, the mediums or "doorkeepers" of the spirit world. Each medium might work with just one or, at the most, a few spirit controls. However, a popular control might turn up at the séances of many mediums. In the late nineteenth century the spirit of John King, supposedly a reformed pirate, and his daughter, Katie King, were claimed as spirit controls by hundreds of mediums.

Spirit controls were notoriously unpredictable. On some occasions they might hold forth with long sermons on morality and philosophy. At other times they might try to answer questions put to them by sitters. But their answers could be incomplete, enigmatic, or downright confusing. The control, if he was in the

Highly imaginative drawing showing the spirit of Katie King materializing at a séance in Philadelphia.

mood, would also help to locate other spirits in his world, and relay messages. For example, he might say, "I have a message for Mrs. Smith, from her husband Henry. He says he is happy on this side and she should not worry."

In some cases the control might actually put another spirit "on"—that is, allow "Henry" to take direct control of the medium. On occasion, an evil spirit, or a severely troubled one, might appear to wrest control of the medium from her regular spirit control. This was a moment of peril, for the agitated spirit could cause the medium to throw herself about and be injured.

As a medium passed from spirit to spirit, her voice would alter, sometimes slightly—sometimes drastically. Some mediums actually appeared to change physically, as different spirits took control of their bodies.

Voice was only one method by which the spirits might communicate. Another was automatic writing. The medium would write out a message under spirit control or direction. Usually the medium had to be in a trance to do any automatic writing, though some claimed to write under spirit control while in a perfectly ordinary state of consciousness. Many persons in addition to mediums have claimed to have done automatic writing.

An enormous number of books, supposedly written under spirit control, flowed from the spiritualist movement.

Like the physical phenomena, many were impressed by the psychic phenomena produced by the mental mediums. Many others, however, including convinced spiritualists, were made quite uncomfortable by much of this alleged spirit communication. A spiritualist named Epes Sargent registered his disbelief in much of what he heard in séances:

"The puerile character of many of the communications for which a spiritual origin is claimed, the reckless assumption of the names of great men and women by pretended spirits, the author of some imbecile doggeral claiming to be Shakespeare, the designer of some atrocious picture signing himself Michael Angelo, and the utterer of some stupid commonplace asking us to believe he is Lord Bacon—of course make the spiritual pretensions of the communicants ridiculous in the estimation of most persons of taste."

Thus with the spirit communications, as with the physical phenomena, intelligent and discerning spiritualists were suspicious of much, but remained convinced that there was a "core of truth" among all the fakery and nonsense.

Who attended séances? For a while it seemed as though practically everybody did. The Emperor Louis Napoleon of France had repeated séances at the Tuileries with his favorite medium, Daniel Dunglas Home. The Tsar of Russia attended séances with Home and with the Fox sisters. Abraham Lincoln was said to have been a spiritualist. This is probably an exaggeration, but Lincoln, like most other intelligent men in America, was at least intrigued by the new movement.

Séances were being held in palaces and farm houses, mansions and shacks. Many clergymen were appalled by activities that they regarded as unorthodox, irreligious, if not downright diabolical. One antispiritualist clergyman reported that the spirits had told him they were agents of the Devil. Many other clergymen flocked enthusiastically to the new movement. To them it appeared to provide scientific backing for religious beliefs. Many of the messages from the spirits were distinctly religious in character and not at all unorthodox. Such messages could have been read as sermons from any pulpit in America without upsetting the congregation.

Clergymen thus assumed the leadership of the factions both for and against spiritualism.

Many scientists, probably most, denounced spiritualism as foolishness and fraud, and they saw it as a shocking return to prescientific ignorance and superstition. They wanted nothing to do with the whole business. But others were less sure. Many attended séances in a mood of open-minded curiosity. Some were disappointed by what they saw and heard. But others left impressed, and feeling even more puzzled than before. A few scientists openly entered the spiritualist movement, others determined to investigate spiritualism and its claims more closely. But how to do it?—that was the problem. The spirits, if indeed there were any, were elusive, and the mediums themselves maddeningly untrustworthy. If the subject were to be investigated it would take cleverness, and great patience.

99

5

The Mediums and the Magicians

You might imagine that a reasonably intelligent and observant person could not be tricked by a fake medium. But you would be quite wrong. Intelligent and observant people were tricked all the time, often just because they believed that they could not be tricked.

Consider the case of the Hungarian physical medium Laszlo Laszlo. Laszlo was billed as "the wonder of the age." His specialty was producing ectoplasm. Ectoplasm was supposed to be the basic material of which ghosts and spirits were made. It was defined by spiritualists as "a subtle living matter present in the physical body, primarily invisible but capable of assuming vaporous liquid or solid states. It is extruded usually in the dark, from the pores and various orifices of the body, is slightly luminous. . ." When a spirit took control of a medium it might be able to produce a likeness of itself, or part of itself, or at the very least a luminous cloud from the ectoplasm contained in the medium's body. So ran spiritualist theory anyway.

The whole idea of ectoplasm was highly suspect by those who were not convinced spiritualists. Many mediums had been caught smuggling quantities of cheesecloth treated with a luminous dye

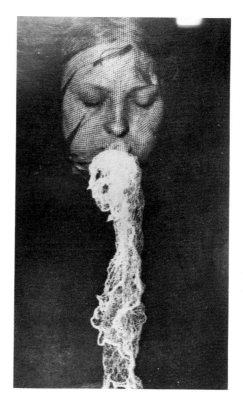

Ectoplasm being extruded from the mouth of a medium.

into their séances. In the dark the luminous cheesecloth looked like what ectoplasm was supposed to look like. Many said that there was no such thing as ectoplasm at all—that it was all luminous cheesecloth. Naturally Laszlo Laszlo was suspected of faking. But no one had ever caught him at it.

Laszlo attracted the attention of Baron von Schrenck-Notzing, a leading psychiatrist of his day who decided to give the medium a thorough investigation. The baron devised an impressive set of controls to keep Laszlo Laszlo from faking. Before each séance he had the medium stripped, bathed, and minutely examined. He even had the medium drink oils that cleaned out his stomach. Schrenck-Notzing wanted to make absolutely certain that Laszlo wasn't sneaking any luminous cheesecloth into the séance.

After all this was over Laszlo was given a robe, which had also been thoroughly searched, and led to the room in which the séance was to be conducted. Even here Laszlo was carefully controlled. He had to conduct his séance from inside a cage.

The first night nothing happened, and Laszlo complained that the vibrations were bad. But on the second night, after going through exactly the same procedure, Laszlo managed to produce clouds of glowing ectoplasm in the dark room. He was equally successful on every other night that he was tested by Baron Schrenck-Notzing.

Was Laszlo Laszlo a real medium? No, he wasn't. He was a fake, as he later admitted. How did he manage to fool people so completely? He had many methods, but the one that he used on Schrenck-Notzing was beautifully simple—and effective. He used the first night, the night on which nothing happened in the séance, to observe the procedure of the test and the baron's habits closely.

On the night of the second test Laszlo Laszlo arrived with a small ball of treated cheesecloth, his ectoplasm, in his pocket. Before he was taken away to be searched and bathed he slipped the cheesecloth into Schrenck-Notzing's pocket. When Laszlo returned, dressed in his robe, he picked the baron's pocket, then he went into his cage and performed his wonders.

From this you can see that investigating the claims of spiritualist mediums was not as easy as it might first appear to be.

Those who undertook the investigation of spiritualist phenomena generally fell into two categories. First there were the skeptics. These were individuals who assumed that all spiritualism was a fraud and that the only problem was to catch the villians red-handed. Among the skeptics were some scientists, particularly psychologists, and many professional magicians. The magicians were especially incensed by the physical mediums, who they thought were simply practicing stage illusions under false pretenses. The magicians were also particularly good at catching frauds because they were professionals at fooling people themselves and they knew just what to look for.

The second category of investigators were the psychical researchers. They were scientists, philosophers, clergymen, and others who were inclined to believe some of the spiritualist claims, but refused to accept them on blind faith. They believed

Sir William Crookes, noted scientist and psychical researcher, tests a "spirit" during a séance. Figure on the floor is the entranced medium.

that these claims should be investigated, sympathetically but honestly, and thoroughly. The first organized group of psychical researchers, The British Society for Psychical Research (S.P.R.), was founded in 1882 by a group of very respectable men, mainly college professors. One of the principle aims of this group was to investigate the alleged contacts between the world of the living and the world of the dead, made by the spiritualists. An American branch of the S.P.R. was formed a few years later.

Some of the psychical researchers were credulous fools. They would believe almost anything, so long as it seemed to lend support to the existence of a spirit world. Such individuals were easily tricked, because they wanted to be tricked. A few became little more than accomplices of crooked mediums. But other psychical researchers, while they were more patient and polite than the skeptics, were just as effective in exposing frauds.

The case of Eusapia Palladino offers a good look at how mediums and psychical researchers of the late nineteenth and early twentieth century worked.

Eusapia Palladino was a poor Italian peasant girl who had become famous in her native land as a medium. She had once been married to a magician so she was immediately suspected of trickery. But she managed to disarm many of her critics. Most mediums disliked investigation of any kind—unless, of course, they were able to dictate all the conditions under which they were to be investigated. The great Palladino was different; she actually seemed to welcome investigation.

But Eusapia Palladino wasn't an easy person to investigate. She was extremely emotional and active. During a séance she groaned and moaned and trembled and sometimes fell on the floor in convulsions. When the séance was over she seemed so exhausted that she was barely able to raise a glass of water to her lips. A person who was moving about as violently as Eusapia always did was hard to watch. Besides she had a very bad temper. At any moment she might throw a tantrum and walk out of a séance.

Palladino captivated Cesare Lombroso, the most famous criminologist of the time. Lombroso had been skeptical of all spiritualism, but Palladino converted him. Marie Curie and her husband Pierre, the discoverers of radium, and another Nobel prize winner, Charles Richet, attended Palladino's séances and went away puzzled and amazed.

Reports of Palladino's triumphs reached the S.P.R. in London. The society had been in operation for over ten years, and by that time the members had investigated so many fraudulent physical mediums that they were pretty soured on the whole class. Still they could not ignore a medium of Palladino's stature. In 1895 the group invited her to England for a series of test sittings at Cambridge. One of those who attended these tests was Richard Hodgson, a professional psychical researcher who worked for the American branch of the S.P.R. Hodgson knew a good deal about stage magic and quickly concluded that Palladino was a fraud. Others who attended the séances, including Professor Henry Sidgwick, first president of the S.P.R. and a firm believer in psychic phenomena, agreed that she was faking. The British researchers were even more shocked to discover that not only did Palladino fake her séances, she even cheated while playing croquet!

But the psychical researchers were polite. They didn't even publish a complete report of their findings. So Palladino went back to Italy and went right on impressing people. Eight years after the first S.P.R. investigation, her reputation had grown so great that the group decided to investigate her again. They sent

105

Eusapia Palladino, the flamboyant physical medium

a three-man commission to Naples, and this time the investigators found no evidence of trickery.

One of the members of the commission was Hereward Carrington, a British-born investigator who lived in the United States. Carrington had been studying physical mediums for years, and had concluded that every one of them had been fraudulent. That was before he encountered Palladino. She was different, he thought, and he was fired with a desire to bring her to the United States.

Finally he was able to arrange a trip and in November of 1909 the great Palladino set out for the United States aboard an Italian liner. Naturally she was recognized immediately, and was induced to hold a séance aboard ship. The newspaper reports of the shipboard séance were sensational. According to the papers, a Dr. Oteri asked to see the spirit of his father.

"In answer to my call we were all overcome by the filmy manifestation that rested on my right shoulder. It was the head of a man, but I did not recognize it as anyone I had ever known. I do not remember my father very well. The impression I got from the manifestation was that it was ghastly, horrible, unexplainable, mysterious."

Another sitter wished to reach his dead mother. He felt something make the sign of the cross. "I distinctly felt the touch on my forehead, then on my breast, and then on each shoulder. . . After that I distinctly felt a kiss on my lips, and after that two kisses on my right cheek."

These advance reports created tremendous interest and the press practically overwhelmed Palladino when she landed in New York. Her first public séances were huge successes. A professional magician who attended one of the séances as Carrington's guest was quite convinced that the medium produced all her phenomena like raps and table tipping by trickery. But he was not able to prove this.

One of the sitters who attended a séance was Hugo Munsterberg, a professor of psychology at Harvard University. Later Carrington must certainly have regretted inviting Munsterberg, for the professor was not one of those polite psychical researchers. He was a hard-nosed skeptic and he was not above employing a little trickery himself.

Another one of the sitters, a man named Edgar Scott, was working with Munsterberg. The light in this séance was provided by a single bulb, wrapped in red tissue paper, and the illumination was so poor that Scott was able to slip, unseen, from his seat and crawl onto the floor behind the medium.

As Munsterberg felt what was supposed to be the spirit hand of John King tugging at his pants leg, Scott on the floor saw that the tugging was being done by the medium's naked foot, which she had slipped out of her boot.

107

A materialized spirit entity that was supposed to have appeared frequently at séances conducted by Pastor Martin Liljeblad.

After watching this performance for a few moments Scott reached over and grabbed Palladino's foot. Wrote Munsterberg: "Then suddenly came a wild, yelling scream. It was a scream as I never heard before in my life, not even in Sarah Bernhardt's most thrilling scenes. It was a scream as if a dagger had stabbed Eusapia right through the heart."

Munsterberg wrote up his experience with Palladino in a magazine article. Carrington may have been a bit shaken, but his faith in the Italian medium was far from destroyed. As we pointed out before, those who believed in spiritualism had long since come to the conclusion that mediums were untrustworthy, and that even the best of them cheated sometime. Besides, Carrington didn't entirely believe Professor Munsterberg's story. But even if it were true he contended it would "merely prove that she had attempted fraud on this particular occasion."

Eusapia Palladino was nothing if not bold. She was undaunted by Munsterberg's exposure. Her tricks had been exposed many times before, yet she had prospered. So early in 1910, Palladino agreed to a series of sittings arranged by Dickinson Miller of Columbia University. A number of scientists participated in the first sittings. All of them agreed that Palladino was cheating, but none of them were exactly sure how she worked her tricks.

Miller then arranged to have some professional magicians attend the séances. The medium was told that the magicians were college professors, so that she would not become suspicious. College professors are easier to fool than magicians. The two séances held with the magicians must have puzzled Palladino herself.

Two of the magicians were employed to hold Palladino's hands and feet during the séance. It was customary during tests of Palladino to have sitters hold her hands and feet to make sure that she was not cheating. However, Palladino could easily free a hand or foot from an ordinary person, without that person ever being aware of it. But she could not free herself from the grasp of professional magicians who knew all the tricks. At first the magicians maintained a loose grip on the medium. During that period the "spirit" raps were heard and the table floated. Then Miller coughed softly. This was a prearranged signal and the magicians tightened their grip. All the manifestations ceased. On another signal the magicians loosened up again, and again the "spirits" were active. The medium surely must have wondered what was going on.

Palladino's greatest surprise, however, would have come when she read an account of these séances published a few weeks later. Only then would she have discovered that two men, one a magician and the other a Columbia University student—both clad in black overalls and black hoods—had crawled into the séance room after the lights were dimmed. These two undercover men had hidden under the chairs of two sitters. They had actually seen the medium kick the table leg to produce "spirit raps," and lift the table with her feet and hands.

The Columbia exposures were widely publicized. Carrington's faith in Palladino, however, remained as firm as ever. He brought in his own magician who testified that the medium could never have produced the effects that he had observed by trickery. The medium's opponents countered by saying that they could do anything that Palladino could do under similar conditions. After a great deal of haggling, a contest between the medium and a magician named Joseph F. Rinn, who was one of the men hidden under the table, was arranged. Palladino never showed up.

Rinn was triumphant. The bold Eusapia Palladino had lost her nerve. She refused to fight. Rinn finally challenged Palladino with a simple test. If she could get the spirits to raise an ordinary pencil a few inches above a table he would give her $2,000. Palladino ignored him.

When Eusapia Palladino finally sailed back to Italy in the middle of 1910, her reputation was not nearly as high as it had been when she first arrived in America. Back in Italy, some of those who had once been astounded by Palladino read of her American fiasco. Now they knew how the tricks had been done. When they attended her séances again they knew what to look for and her deceptions became obvious. A lot of people were very embarrassed when they learned they had been taken in, in the first place.

Despite the Palladino disaster, and countless other exposures and confessions, many people continued to take physical mediumship very seriously—at least seriously enough to investigate the medium's claims. Nor were all of the investigators convinced spiritualists by any means. The magazine *Scientific American* offered a prize of $5,000 to any medium whom a committee appointed by the magazine would certify as genuine. At first the magazine's offer attracted nothing but a collection of obvious fakers. Then in 1924 the *Scientific American* committee was confronted by the most formidable American medium of that or any other time—Margery.

Margery was the pseudonym of Minna Crandon, the wife of Dr. Le Roi Goddard Crandon, a prominent and wealthy Boston surgeon. For over a year reports of the marvelous phenomena produced in Margery's séances had been circulating in spiritualist circles. In person Mrs. Crandon was an attractive woman in her mid-twenties, with a forceful, almost overpowering personality. What made her mediumship particularly impressive was that unlike Palladino and many others she did not need the money. She seemed to have nothing to gain, and a great deal to lose by cheating.

Until 1924 Margery had not been adequately tested. All her séances had been held in private. But in April, 1924, when Dr. Crandon heard of the *Scientific American* committee, he asked them to come to Boston and investigate his wife. The prize money did not interest the couple; they had plenty. What Dr. Crandon wanted was for the committee to endorse his wife as a genuine medium. He wrote to the magazine and said that he would pay all the expenses of committee members.

Various members of the committee traveled to Boston to attend Margery's séances. They were impressed. It seemed as though they were on the point of publicly giving her their approval. But there was still one member of the committee who had not yet seen Margery—he was the great magician Harry Houdini.

Houdini had become known as the archfoe of fraudulent mediums. Like many other magicians he was angry that mediums seemed to be using the tricks of his trade without acknowledging them. But he was also really interested in physical research, and he hoped that communication between the living and the dead could be established. Houdini continually searched for proof of such communication, and was continually disappointed. This had made him a doubly ferocious opponent of fraud, and he spent a good part of his career as a crusader against spiritualism.

Houdini had once been a close friend of the writer Sir Arthur Conan Doyle, creator of Sherlock Holmes. Like the magician, Sir Arthur too hoped that communication between the living and the dead was possible. But Sir Arthur believed that the proof was already there. He was a convinced spiritualist. His lectures on spiritualism attracted huge audiences and helped convert many to the cause.

Sir Arthur's wife was an amateur medium. At one point Sir Arthur gave Houdini a written message that his wife said she had received from the magician's dead mother. Houdini had always been very close to his mother, and it was the burning desire to contact her that had drawn him to an investigation of spiritualism in the first place. The moment that Houdini looked at the message he knew that something was wrong. The message was written in English, while the magician's mother had been born in Europe and had never learned to write English. Houdini was enraged at what he considered an insult to the memory of his mother. But Sir Arthur blandly replied that Houdini's mother had learned English by going to college in Heaven. This was too much for Houdini and he never spoke to Sir Arthur Conan Doyle again. Sir Arthur concluded that Houdini himself was a medium but perversely denied this fact and slandered all other mediums.

Early in 1924 Harry Houdini had been a very busy man, and it was not until June that he learned of the *Scientific American* committee's investigation of Margery. He was shocked. It seemed to him that the committee was getting ready to give a vote of approval to a medium that he had never even seen. And so the stage was set for a confrontation between two powerful personalities—Houdini the magician and Margery the medium.

From the very first sitting Houdini was sure that Margery was a fraud. Before the séance he had worn a rubber surgical bandage on his knee until the knee was sore and tender. He removed the bandage and rolled up his trouser leg during the séance. His sensitive skin could thus detect any motions of Margery's leg under the table that might have gone undetected through his thick trousers.

Margery, like most fraudulent physical mediums, used her agile feet to produce most of her "phenomena." There was nothing particularly original in her performance, and most of the tricks were obvious to Houdini. "Well, gentlemen," Houdini said to some of his fellow committee members after they left the séance, "I've got her. All fraud, every bit of it. One more sitting and I will be ready to expose everything."

There was only one effect which puzzled Houdini. During the séance, while the medium's hands and feet were being carefully held, she made a megaphone fall on the table in front of him. How had she managed it? After thinking a while Houdini realized

113

Houdini tests Margery at a séance.

that Margery had placed the megaphone on her head before people took control of her hands and feet. The séance room was, of course, quite dark so no one could see what she was doing. Then at the proper moment she merely snapped her head and the megaphone shot off in any direction she desired. With grudging admiration Houdini admitted that this was "the slickest ruse I have ever detected."

But knowing Margery was a fraud, and proving that she was, were two entirely different matters. At least one member of the *Scientific American* committee was still convinced that she was genuine, and others were not sure, but they were certainly not ready to dismiss Margery as a fake, unless Houdini could come up with solid proof.

Houdini constructed what he considered to be a fraudproof

114

box. The medium was to sit in the wooden box with only her head and hands sticking out through round holes. If she could still produce phenomena while seated in this box, Houdini said, then perhaps she was not a fraud. Margery and her husband were a bit taken aback when Houdini showed up for a sitting with his fraudproof box, but after some hesitation they agreed to conduct a séance with Margery seated in the contraption. However, shortly after the séance began the front of the box broke open. Houdini thought that the medium herself had broken it with her shoulders as the box had been lightly constructed, and she could have easily have done so. Dr. Crandon, however, claimed that Walter, Margery's spirit control, had broken the box.

Walter was supposed to be the spirit of Margery's dead brother. He was an unusually blunt-spoken control and during the séances with Houdini, Walter became downright abusive and profane.

Houdini had his fraudproof box reinforced and the séance

Back view of Houdini's fraudproof box for testing Margery

115

began again. "Houdini," Walter's voice growled during the séance, "you are clever indeed, but it won't work."

An argument between Walter and Houdini quickly erupted in the dark room. "Houdini . . . get the hell out of here and never come back. If you don't, I will," Walter shouted. The séance broke up in furious controversy.

When Margery learned that Houdini was going to denounce her publicly as a fraud she first pleaded with him not to do so, for the sake of her son. Then she threatened that her supporters would beat him up. In other séances Walter began predicting the magician's imminent death, and the controls of other mediums echoed the grim prediction. Houdini was unmoved, and he denounced Margery anyway. The whole affair had become very ugly.

The report of the *Scientific American* committee was delayed for a long time. When it finally did come out Houdini repeated his accusations of fraud. Other members, including several who deeply believed in psychic phenomena also admitted that Margery had never demonstrated any supernormal powers under controlled conditions. Only one member of the group, Hereward Carrington, who had been Eusapia Palladino's great supporter, continued to affirm that Margery was a true medium.

The greatest blow to Margery's credibility came not from Houdini but from one of her disillusioned supporters—a man named E. E. Dudley. One of the most impressive feats during Margery's séances was when Walter announced that he would impress his fingerprints in a soft ball of wax. Since the fingerprints did not belong to anyone present in the room it was assumed that they had to belong to the spirit of Walter. But in 1929 Dudley traced the fingerprints. They did not belong to Margery's dead brother but to her dentist, who was very much alive and living in Boston. The dentist was surprised to find that his fingerprints were being passed off as those of a spirit.

Still, so forceful was Margery's personality that she continued to dominate the scene. Up until she came along, the S.P.R. in America had been doing a pretty good job of exposing fraudulent mediums. So good, in fact, that some members complained that they were running a society *against* psychical research. Margery's supporters moved into important positions in the organization. They called for investigation after investigation, and they often refused to publish findings that were detrimental to the medium. Today this period is looked back upon as one of the most unfortunate in the history of psychical research in America.

Margery continued to give séances until 1938. But the circle of those who believed in her powers grew smaller and smaller. Indeed the whole idea of physical mediumship had finally lost its appeal. Margery was the last important physical medium to be carefully investigated.

There are still physical mediums today—but they do not seek to convince investigation committees of their abilities. They avoid honest investigations, and demonstrate their "powers" only to those who already believe in them.

6

From Beyond the Grave

Eusapia Palladino and Margery were flamboyant and theatrical characters. Their triumphs and their failures made headlines. Their séances were filled with weird noises and flying objects. Mrs. Leonora Piper was greater than either of them, yet she made no headlines and there were no tipping tables or luminous clouds at her séances. There wasn't even the tiniest little spirit rap. Mrs. Piper was a mental medium. She lived during what is now regarded as the golden age of psychical research. One of the reasons that it was golden is that the researchers were able to study Mrs. Piper.

Mrs. Piper, a Boston housewife, got into the mediumship business almost by accident. All of her life she was troubled by illnesses, both real and imaginary. She constantly lugged around a stock of pills, smelling salts, and other medicines, and she trekked from doctor to doctor. But she found no lasting relief for her various complaints. Finally in 1884 she went to see a "psychic healer," a person who claimed to be able to cure disease through some sort of intervention with the spirits. The healer did nothing for Mrs. Piper's health, but during one of the sessions Mrs. Piper went into a trance, and her body was apparently seized by the spirit of a dead Indian maiden with the curious name of Chlorine.

Chlorine wasn't very talkative, and thus made an unsatisfactory control. After a few sessions she departed from Mrs. Piper, and in the séances that followed the entranced medium seemed to come under the control of a variety of spirits. Indeed, there appeared to be a virtual battle royal going on in the spirit world to see who would take control of the body of Mrs. Leonora Piper. As Mrs. Piper began to sink into a trance she was torn by great pain, and some observers believed that the cause of the pain was the ghostly struggle going on for possession of her body. Among the battlers were such well-known figures as the poet Henry Wadsworth Longfellow and the composer Johann Sebastian Bach. But the eventual winner of the struggle was an unknown French physician named Phinuit.

Dr. Phinuit seemed to have a definite personality, but there were some difficulties regarding his spirit. No one was ever able to find any record that such an individual had ever lived. Moreover, this French doctor didn't speak very much French and knew next to nothing about medicine. Dr. Phinuit explained that he had lived so long in the English colony at Marseille that he had all but forgotten his native tongue. Like all controls, Dr. Phinuit was temperamental and unreliable. He often failed to respond to difficult questions, or gave answers that were incomplete, just plain gibberish, or simply wrong.

Still, during séances with Mrs. Piper, Dr. Phinuit seemed to possess information about some of the sitters that should not have been known to the medium by any normal means. Mrs. Piper began to develop a substantial reputation.

In 1885 Mrs. Piper came to the attention of the great American psychologist, William James, of Harvard. James had a deep

119

Leonora Piper, the celebrated mental medium

interest in psychic phenomena, and was one of the founders of the American branch of the Society for Psychical Research. James was very impressed by Mrs. Piper and suggested to Richard Hodgson, then president of the S.P.R., that an extensive investigation of the medium be undertaken.

Hodgson was an experienced and tough-minded investigator of psychic phenomena, and one of the best psychical researchers in history. He admitted that he had a strong wish to believe in contact with the spirit world, but he was contemptuous of frauds. Before he began his investigation of Mrs. Piper, Hodgson had written a devastating report on his investigation of that exotic faker, Madame Helena Petrovena Blavatsky. Even while his long investigation of Mrs. Piper was going on, Hodgson helped to ruin the reputation of Eusapia Palladino. He was no fool, and was a man whose opinion has to be taken seriously, even today.

The tests Hodgson arranged seemed simple and foolproof. He would assemble a group of sitters who were presumably unknown to the medium. He would then introduce them to her under false names and give no indication of their backgrounds, or anything else about them. Then during the séance Dr. Phinuit would give details about the sitters or about some of their dead relatives and friends. Before and after séances Hodgson often had Mrs. Piper followed, just to make sure that she wasn't trying to find out anything about the sitters. In fact, Mrs. Piper became virtually a prisoner, though a willing one, of Hodgson and the S.P.R.

It might seem that tests like this would be absolutely conclusive. Either Mrs. Piper could produce information about the lives of her anonymous sitters, or she couldn't. But, as with everything else in the field of psychical research, it didn't turn out to be that simple. The alleged spirit of Dr. Phinuit didn't just rattle off information like a computer. He rambled on; he was vague and elusive on many points; he asked a lot of leading questions, often contradicted himself, and made many glaring errors. He did not answer direct questions, but rather volunteered whatever information he wanted. During it all, however, Dr. Phinuit seemed to come up with some startling facts. At one sitting he appeared to give a detailed description of a sitter's father, but he got the name wrong, attributing the real name of the sitter himself to the description of his own father.

Lengthy transcripts of many of these séances are available. Different people get different impressions from reading them. Some feel that Mrs. Piper was either in contact with the spirit world or possessed some other uncanny ability to gain information through channels other than the normal sensory ones. Others who have read the transcripts are not at all impressed, and say that Mrs. Piper was just more skilled at fishing for information than most mediums.

After two years of testing, Hodgson himself came to the conclusion that Mrs. Piper was a medium who was far above the mass of frauds and fakers he had investigated in the past. He had a growing suspicion that there really might be something to the spiritualism business after all. But he wanted more tests.

Hodgson suggested that the British S.P.R. invite the medium to England. Mrs. Piper had never been out of America, and Hodgson believed that her lack of previous knowledge about England and its people would make testing conditions there ideal.

On shipboard Mrs. Piper was kept secluded and upon her arrival in England was met by Oliver Lodge, professor of physics and an ardent psychical investigator. Professor Lodge allowed the medium to talk to no one and rushed her in a closed carriage to his own home where she was kept virtually under lock and key. The servants in the house were temporary replacements, for Lodge feared that some of the usual household staff might let slip some information that would be useful to the medium. All family records, pictures, or anything else that might provide Mrs. Piper with background information was carefully hidden.

Then there began a series of séances that resembled those conducted by Hodgson in America. Anonymous sitters were brought to the séances and Mrs. Piper repeated her previous successes. The members of the British Society for Psychical Research were very impressed. Lodge himself was particularly struck by Mrs. Piper since, through her spirit control, she had apparently been able to reveal some information about his family that not even he had known. After checking it out, it proved to be true.

After her return to America, Mrs. Piper began a series of séances upon which most of her reputation rests. These séances featured a spirit who called himself G. P. This G. P. was supposed to be George Pellew, a young English friend of Hodgson who had died suddenly in February of 1892. Sometime before his death, Pellew had attended a séance with Mrs. Piper (under a false name, of course) but he had apparently not been very impressed. He seemed to have no particular significance in the life of Mrs. Piper.

A few weeks after Pellew's death, another of his friends attended a Piper séance and, as was customary, was introduced under a false name. In the middle of the séance the voice of Dr. Phinuit suddenly said, "There is another George who wants to speak to you." The voice coming from the medium altered as the new spirit took control. This spirit introduced himself as G. P. and revealed some information both about Pellew and the sitter.

Many friends of the dead George Pellew were brought to the séances. They were struck not only by how much G. P. seemed to know about them and about Pellew, but by how much the voice coming from Mrs. Piper resembled Pellew's.

Dr. Phinuit did not disappear. In fact, during séances he did most of the talking. G. P. customarily communicated by automatic writing. Mrs. Piper would be slumped over in a deep trance. She would speak in the voice of Dr. Phinuit, while her hand furiously wrote out messages from G. P. The total effect was very eerie.

These strange proceedings continued night after night for months. One of the most significant incidents in the series took

123

place during the winter of 1892. Attending the séance was James Howard who had been a close friend of Pellew's. Hodgson was recording the events. Mrs. Piper was in a deep trance, her body was completely limp and, to all outward appearances—lifeless.

Howard had attended several séances already, but he was not convinced that he was in contact with the spirit of his dead friend. "Tell me," he demanded, "something known only to G. P. and myself."

The medium's hand began to twitch. She grabbed a pencil and started writing at great speed. Hodgson picked up the sheets and read them aloud as she finished. Howard agreed that the information on them was generally correct. Then the medium wrote the word "Private" and pushed Hodgson away.

"I retired to the other side of the room, and Mr. Howard took my place close to the hand where he could read the writing. He did not, of course, read it aloud and it was too private for my perusal. The hand, as it reached the end of each sheet, tore it off from the block book, and thrust it wildly at Mr. Howard, and then continued writing. The circumstances narrated, Mr. Howard informed me, contained precisely the kind of test for which he had asked, and he said that he was 'perfectly satisfied, perfectly.'"

But Hodgson was not yet perfectly satisfied. He gathered thirty more of George Pellew's friends, none of whom was presumably known to the medium. He then brought in 120 other people. He wanted to see if the spirit of G. P. could identify Pellew's friends from a group of total strangers. G. P. picked out every one of the thirty, without a mistake. G. P. was also said to have given information about the location of a tin box of Pellew's private papers which was supposedly lost after his death.

Richard Hodgson, pioneer psychic investigator

Finally the skeptical Hodgson himself was converted to spiritualism. He really became convinced that he was in the presence of the spirit of his old friend George Pellew speaking and writing through Mrs. Leonora Piper. Hodgson wrote, "I cannot profess to have any doubt but that they . . . have survived the change we call death, and they have direct communication with us whom we call living, through Mrs. Piper's entranced organism."

Hodgson's conversion to spiritualism, however, did not destroy his critical abilities. During this period he was busily exposing Eusapia Palladino, and others.

In January, 1906, Richard Hodgson suddenly and unexpec-

125

tedly dropped dead while playing handball. This man who had played such an important part in the development of psychical research was to do an encore for the field after his death. He was to appear as a spirit control. The "spirit" of Hodgson was first heard in séances being conducted by a British medium living in India. But soon he popped up as the spirit control of Mrs. Piper herself.

Hodgson had been a brilliant psychical researcher, but as a spirit control he was rather a failure. Many of George Pellew's friends were impressed that when G. P. was speaking through Mrs. Piper, they were really in contact with the spirit of George Pellew. Most of Hodgson's friends did not feel the same way about the Hodgson control. William James said that these sessions revealed nothing that Mrs. Piper could not have learned during her association with the living Hodgson. Oliver Lodge was similarly disappointed.

Mrs. Piper's mediumistic career was going downhill. Though she was to continue to give séances for many more years, and was to have a few more brilliant moments, her performance was to become more erratic and unsatisfactory. The Hodgson control was ultimately ousted by a series of famous historical figures like Julius Caesar and George Eliot. Finally she was taken over by the Imperator Band, which was supposed to be a tribe of ancient phantoms that had appeared to other mediums. It was hard to take her seriously anymore.

Still, there were her early years, and most notably the period when G. P. was her control. Did the spirit of the dead George Pellew speak through the body of Mrs. Piper? Richard Hodgson thought so, and many of Pellew's other friends agreed. But Pellew's family emphatically did not. His parents flatly denied that the material reported at Mrs. Piper's séances had anything to do with their dead son. His mother denounced G. P.'s communications as "utter drivel and inanity."

The dead man's brother, C. E. Pellew, a professor of literature at Columbia University, complained of the "absolute unreliability of any statement of the believers in the Mrs. Piper cult." He said that the famous tin box located by G. P. was in fact empty, and that the "missing" papers had been in the possession of a friend since George Pellew's death.

In a letter C. E. Pellew wrote, "I was finally persuaded to see Mrs. Piper, and found her a bright, shrewd, ill-educated, commonplace woman who answered glibly enough questions where guessing was easy, or where she might have obtained previous information. But whenever I asked anything that would be known only to George himself, she was either silent or entirely wrong."

Who was right? Was Mrs. Piper really in the control of the spirit of George Pellew, as Hodgson and many of the dead man's friends believed? Or was Mrs. Piper merely a faker as Pellew's family and others seemed to imply? Or did the truth lie somewhere in-between?

Mrs. Piper's trances seemed real enough, but if she was not being controlled by outside spirits what was happening to her? Many psychiatrists and indeed many psychical researchers believe the "controls" of mediums are not outside spirits, but unconscious parts of the medium's own personality. The entranced medium will actually be controlled, but the "spirit" that does the controlling will be part of the medium's own personality. This is something like a split personality. Some mediums have been given psychological tests both while awake and in a trance, and the tests seem to bear out this theory.

Mrs. Piper, herself, suspected that there was something wrong with her own mind. She always denied that she was a spiritualist, or that she had any proof that the spirits spoke through her body. When she was asked why she had spent so much time working with the Society for Psychical Research she replied, "Because of my desire to learn if I were possessed or obsessed."

If Mrs. Piper was not controlled by a spirit, how did she know some of the extraordinary things that she seemed to know about her sitters? One explanation is that she really didn't know anything out of the ordinary; that people who wanted to believe they were in touch with the dead interpreted her vague statements as being much more significant than they really were. In short, many believed that Mrs. Piper was a fraud, an unconscious fraud perhaps, but a fraud nonetheless.

A second explanation is that Mrs. Piper and other mediums like her were gifted with extrasensory perception (ESP)—that they could read other people's minds. Thus, they could have picked up the information from the minds of their living sitters, rather than from communication with the dead. In this way Mrs. Piper could know a good deal about the friends of George Pellew, simply by reading their minds as they sat in the séance. The whole subject of ESP itself is highly controversial. Most scientists do not believe that the existence of ESP has been adequately established. Most psychical researchers, on the other hand, tend to believe in ESP even when they do not believe in spirits. So you can see how the belief in ESP complicated the already difficult attempt to establish the possibility of communication with the spirit world.

In the 1880's, when organized psychical research first began, its founders felt that the claims of spiritualism could be established or disproved quickly. Over a quarter of a century later the researchers were still tormented by the same doubts and uncertainties, and driven to further investigation by the same hopes they had when they started. Obviously the problem was not going to be nearly as easy as they had first assumed. By this time some of the pioneers of psychical research had died, or "passed over to the other side," as the spiritualists might say. If there was indeed a spirit world, and if communication between the living and dead was possible, what spirits would be more interested in establishing this communication than the spirits of the psychical research founders themselves? They had, after all, spent a good part of their lives making the attempt. After they were dead, it was reasoned, they might continue to try to establish communication, but this time from "the other side." Therefore, it is not surprising that the spirits of some of the psychical research pioneers began showing up as controls at various séances. A prime example was the Richard Hodgson control of Mrs. Piper.

During the early years of the twentieth century, the departed founders of psychical research seemed to be engaged in a vast worldwide word game. The result was that extraordinary series of communications that came to be known as "the cross-correspondences." A few weeks after the death of Frederic Myers, one of the founders of the S.P.R., a medium who worked regularly for the group began getting messages from Myers' spirit. Soon other mediums who had worked with the S.P.R., including Mrs. Piper, began getting messages from Myers and other prominent members of the group who had died. Most of the messages were recorded by automatic writing, and the communication continued on and off for some thirty years. To many psychical researchers it seemed as though Myers and the others were frantically attempting to establish their survival by sending complex messages from beyond the grave.

The special feature of this communication was that there were many references to the same topic, or "cross-correspondence," in the messages received by different mediums. Since the mediums lived in different parts of the world there seemed little chance that they were in collusion with one another, to construct these complicated interlocking messages. If such messages could not be attributed to fraud or coincidence then they would have to be regarded as proof that the mediums were being controlled from "the other side" by the spirits of the psychical researchers.

Myers and his friends had been literary scholars and the topic chosen for a "cross-correspondence" was usually a literary one. Here, according to D. J. West, a member of the Society for Psychical Research is "an extremely simple example of a cross-correspondence." It is called the "Laurel Wreath" case.

"One day Mrs. Piper, when in a trance, repeated the word 'laurel' several times." Next day, when supposedly controlled by the spirit of F. W. H. Myers, she said, "I gave Mrs. Verrall [another medium] laurel wreath . . . An examination of her [Mrs. Verrall's] script showed that on an occasion three weeks before she had written 'Apollo's laurel bough,' 'Laureatus,' 'A laurel wreath,' *'corona laureta,'* and various other references to laurel and laurel wreath." Again, three weeks after Mrs. Piper's reference to laurel, Mrs. Verrall's script contained "Laurel leaves are emblem. Laurel for the victor's brow."

We must stress that this is an extremely *simple* example. More typically the cross-correspondences involved dozens of references, allusions to obscure phrases, and so forth. West comments that it, "looked like deliberate attempts to set the investigators a puzzle." Over the thirty years that the cross-correspondences were being produced the mediums turned out hundreds of thousands of pages of automatic writing. At least one man (J. G. Piddington) spent most of his life studying them, and trying to make some order out of this overwhelming mass of material.

Some serious psychical researchers consider the cross-correspondence the best evidence ever for communication from beyond the grave. Others are not nearly so enthusiastic. They think that the thousands upon thousands of pages of cross-correspondence are just too complicated and that some researchers were seeing "significant" messages that were not there. In such a huge mass of materials there would be many perfectly ordinary coincidental linkings of words, as in the "Laurel Wreath" case. Skeptics dismiss the entire mass of cross-correspondence as empty words.

While this vast and complex series of communications was going on, other messages, supposedly from dead psychical researchers, were also coming through. A medium might be told to refer to a particular page of a particular book. Something on that page was supposed to have some reference to the life on earth of the spirit communicator. But, as usual, the information was vague, and open to all sorts of interpretation. Those who did not believe in spirit communication found them too inconclusive to be of any value. Those who had always been uncertain of spirit communication remained uncertain. No one's mind had been changed. The elusive spirits remained as elusive as ever.

Living psychical researchers began to wonder. Why, if their deceased predecessors were trying to "get through," did they have to be so very complicated about it, when a simple message would do just as well? A simple message—that seemed to be the key. But it had to be a message that would not be known to any living person, and thus the possibility of fraud or ESP would be eliminated. Psychical researchers began leaving secret sealed messages. After the investigator's death, his spirit would try to communicate this message from "the other side."

This plan sounds fine—in theory. But there is one big hitch in it. Let us say that a medium gets what she believes is the secret message from a spirit. In order to find out whether she has gotten the correct message, the dead man's sealed message must be opened. If the medium's message turns out to be wrong the value of the sealed message as a test has been destroyed anyway, because now a lot of people know what it said, and the door has been opened to fakers. All of these attempts to send messages proved to be disappointments.

Then early in 1929 it seemed as though an authentic and undeniable message from the dead had been received. The spirit sending the message was not a psychical researcher, but rather that archfoe of spirit mediums, Harry Houdini the magician.

As we have said, Houdini himself was vitally interested in proving communication with the dead. Before he died he was said to have agreed to try to communicate some sort of coded message to his wife, Beatrice. He was also said to have left sealed messages for other friends in a bank vault. These too he would try to communicate after his death, according to the stories that circulated.

The great magician died in 1926, appropriately enough on Halloween. Houdini's widow offered $10,000 for proof of communication with her dead husband. She was deluged with messages from spirit mediums, but they had no meaning to her. Ultimately she withdrew the reward offer. However, one message, supposedly received by a New York medium named Arthur Ford, seemed a bit out of the ordinary. The message was not said to have come from Houdini himself, but rather from the magician's mother. It concerned a private matter in Houdini's family.

The medium might easily have found out about this family incident by perfectly normal means. Houdini's wife had written of it to Sir Arthur Conan Doyle, and Ford knew Sir Arthur. Also a newspaper had once published something about this matter shortly after Houdini's death.

So the message produced by Arthur Ford wasn't much, but it was something. At least it brought the medium to the attention of Houdini's widow.

In January of 1929 the newspapers reported that Houdini's widow was very ill, and that while semidelirious believed that she was in touch with the spirit of her husband. A week later, before she had recovered from her illness, Mrs. Houdini held a séance with Arthur Ford. Present were some of Ford's friends, a couple of newspaper reporters, and Mrs. Houdini's friend and nurse.

Ford went into a trance and his spirit guide Fletcher took over. Fletcher was then replaced by a voice that identified itself as "Houdini." The Houdini voice relayed a coded message. When translated it came to one word—"believe." Beatrice agreed that it was the correct message.

The Houdini voice ended the séance by saying, "Spare no time or money to undo my attitude of doubt while on earth . . . Give yourself to placing the truth before all those who have lost the faith, and want to take hold . . . Tell the world, sweetheart, that Harry Houdini lives and will prove it a thousand times."

Naturally the story of this séance created a sensation. Newspapers all over the world carried the news of the great Houdini's return from the grave. Reporters flocked to talk to Mrs. Houdini.

She affirmed that the story was true, and that as soon as she was well again she would take them to the bank vault in which Houdini's coded message to her and the messages for others had been placed.

Houdini's old enemy, Margery the medium, smelled revenge. "Harry Houdini, in death, has furnished the world with the evidence which conclusively refutes the theories which he so vigorously defended in life," she crowed.

Not everyone who knew Houdini was convinced that he had spoken from "the other side." Houdini's brother stated that the séance was a fraud. Joseph Dunninger, a magician associate of Houdini, pointed out that the "mysterious" Houdini code, was no mystery at all. It was a code that Houdini and his wife had once used in their act. The key to the code was well known by theater people, and in fact it had been printed in a biography of Houdini published shortly after his death. It would not have been hard for Arthur Ford to have learned of this code, by perfectly normal means.

Mrs. Houdini clouded the issue by indicating that the decoded word "believe" had come as a surprise to her. She did not know what word was to be transmitted. All she knew was the code.

Just two days after the séance, the New York *Graphic* headlined, HOUDINI MESSAGE A BIG HOAX! In the story one of the reporters who had covered the original séance said that Ford had admitted that Mrs. Houdini had given him the code, and that the two of them were planning a lecture tour. Two other employees of the newspaper, who had been hiding nearby affirmed that this indeed was what Ford had said.

Ford denied everything, and threatened legal action. Mrs. Houdini also denied taking part in any hoax. The air was filled with charges and countercharges, but nothing was ever really resolved.

Mrs. Houdini never showed the messages from her husband that were supposed to be in a sealed vault. After she recovered she continually denied that she had ever received any communication from her husband through Arthur Ford or any other medium. Ford himself never claimed to have received any other messages from Houdini, and in later years he didn't talk much about the Houdini code.

Mrs. Houdini did not give up trying to contact her husband after this incident. Each Halloween, the anniversary of Houdini's death, she would sit in front of his lighted portrait, hoping that a message would come through. Nothing happened. Finally after ten years she turned off the light on his portrait. "Houdini hasn't come," she said. "I don't believe he will come."

Though all the principals in the case—Arthur Ford, Beatrice Houdini, as well as Harry Houdini himself—are now dead, the controversy over the Houdini message lives on. As is usual, people believe whatever version suits them.

But neither the Houdini message, nor any of the other messages "from beyond the grave" has provided the ironclad proof that the psychical researchers have been looking for.

7

Haunted Houses and Poltergeists

Any house that is old and deserted is likely to acquire the reputation of being haunted. If something violent or strange like a murder or suicide once took place in the house, so much the better (or worse) for its haunted reputation.

You have probably walked through a house that was supposed to be haunted, or at least seen one from the outside. But most houses that are called haunted get that reputation simply because they look like they should be haunted. There is really nothing about them that calls for further investigation. However, every once in a while there are things that happen in a house that appear so genuinely odd, that the house attracts the attention of psychical researchers. But these real "haunted houses" rarely resemble the haunted houses of traditional ghost stories. Outwardly, at least, such houses are quite ordinary looking. Let us look at a couple of modern cases.

There was a celebrated ghost that supposedly haunted a house owned by a Broadway columnist named Danton Walker. Now, we must recognize from the start that Danton Walker believed in ghosts. He had already written a great deal about the ghosts that were supposedly haunting this or that famous person, so he

136

was not going to be the most skeptical witness to any ghostly encounter.

In 1942, Walker bought a house in Rockland County, New York. The house was on the Hudson River, about a one-hour drive from New York City where the columnist worked. He didn't intend to live in the house regularly, but he planned to use it for vacations and weekends. The house itself was very old, dating back to pre-Revolutionary War times, and when he first found it, it was badly run down, and needed considerable repair and renovation.

Walker didn't know much about the previous history of the old place, though he had heard rumors that it was haunted. Since such rumors are attached to almost any old and run-down house he paid no attention to them.

The house was located in a part of New York state that was important during the Revolutionary War. The headquarters of General "Mad" Anthony Wayne had stood nearby, and the site of the bloody battle of Stony Point was just a few miles away. The house itself had probably once housed Revolutionary War soldiers, or been used to store equipment or keep prisoners, though there was no definite record of any of this.

From the beginning Walker said that he heard strange noises, and often felt an unseen "presence" when he was in the old place. But it was not until 1944, when the house had been fully restored, and Walker began going to it regularly that ghostly things really began to happen.

Most of the strange happenings were unexplainable noises. According to Walker it sounded as though someone in heavy boots was tramping around rooms that were known to be empty. Occasionally it sounded as though someone were knocking at the door, but when Walker went to answer he found that no one was

137

Nineteenth-century illustrator's conception of the appearance of a ghost

there. No one in the house ever actually reported seeing any
ghostly figures, but there were other manifestations in addition
to the noises. Objects would disappear from their accustomed
place and turn up weeks later in a different part of the house.
Pictures fell mysteriously from the wall. A large pewter pitcher
either fell or was thrown at a woman visitor to the house. Walker
and others were gripped by strange chills. Worst of all there
was the overpowering feeling that "something unearthly" was
in the house. Finally the situation go so bad that the columnist
would no longer spend nights in the house. He slept in a studio
he had constructed behind the main house where he was not
disturbed by the strange goings on.

Oddly enough, despite Danton Walker's interest in ghosts
and hauntings, he didn't try to do anything about his own
haunted house for a full ten years. In 1952 the tales of the
haunted house in Rockland County came to the attention of Mrs.
Eileen Garrett, an Irish medium who lived in America. Until her
death in 1970, Mrs. Garrett was the most respected and responsible medium of modern times. While Mrs. Piper had been es-
sentially an employee of the Society for Psychical Research,
Mrs. Garrett, who was a good businesswoman as well as a good
medium, had her own psychical research group called the Parapsychology Foundation. Mrs. Garrett was always intrigued by
stories of hauntings, and she asked if she could come up and
look into this one. Walker agreed.

On a stormy day in November of 1952, Mrs. Garrett and a
small group from her Parapsychology Foundation made the hour
trip to Danton Walker's haunted house. They carried with them
infrared photography equipment, for taking pictures in the dark,
and a tape recorder. However, the principal tool with which they
hoped to track down the ghost was Mrs. Garrett herself.

139

Mrs. Garrett rarely bothered with the elaborate ritual of the traditional séance. It was the middle of the afternoon when she arrived. After a brief inspection of the house she marched into the living room and sat down in a comfortable chair, while the others gathered around her. The tape recorder was switched on and Mrs. Garret slipped easily into a trance. Almost immediately her East Indian spirit control, Unvani, began speaking through her. He said that he was going to allow another spirit, the spirit that presumably had been haunting Walker's house, take control of the medium. But Unvani warned, "Remember that you are dealing with a personality very young, tired, who has been very much hurt in life. . ."

The change from the dignified and calm Unvani control to this new spirit was startling and grotesque to the observers. Mrs. Garrett's eyes popped wide open and she stared straight ahead, in terror, but it also appeared that she was unable to see anything. Her whole body began to tremble violently and she started moaning and weeping. Then the medium fell out of her chair and tried to drag herself across the floor toward where Walker was seated. When she tried to stand up her leg gave way, as though it was broken. She lay on the floor trembling violently. There were several uncomfortable moments before anyone in the room was able to make contact with this new spirit that was supposed to be controlling the body of the medium. Even then they could get little information, for the spirit seemed confused, in great pain, and spoke very poor English.

What they could gather from the garbled dialogue was that they were supposed to be talking to the spirit of a Polish mercenary named Andreas who had served with the Revolutionary army. He had been carrying some sort of map when he was trapped by the British soldiers in that very house. They beat him horribly and left him for dead, but he did not die, at least not at once. He lingered on for several terrible, pain-filled days, before finally expiring. The Andreas spirit also made some mention of a brother, but at first no one could make head or tail out of this.

After the story had been told, Unvani again assumed control of the medium. She got up off the floor, bowed, sat down in a chair and, with the voice of Unvani, explained the situation a bit further. He said that Danton Walker resembled the dead man's brother who had also been killed during the Revolutionary War, and it was this resemblance that triggered the haunting after Walker purchased the house.

Unvani suggested that all present pray for the repose of the troubled spirit of the Polish mercenary. After that Mrs. Garrett awoke from her trance and said she was totally unaware of what had been going on. The whole séance had taken an hour and fifteen minutes. A few months after the séance Walker reported that the atmosphere around his house seemed much calmer.

Was this a case of a real ghost in a real haunted house? The problem divides itself into two parts. First there are the noises, the chills, the mysteriously disappearing objects, and other strange events that seemed to happen in this particular house. But are these things so out of the ordinary that we must bring in a ghost to explain them? Old houses are often filled with strange and seemingly unexplainable noises. Stairs creak and windows rattle, but these are perfectly natural. Cracks let in drafts and create sudden chills. All of us have had the momentary feeling that there is something strange or unearthly in the house with us. How often have you had the experience of putting down an object, and returned to get it later, only to find that it had disappeared? Was the object carried away by a ghost, or was the dis-

141

appearance the result of carelessness or forgetfulness? If you believed strongly in ghosts you might attribute all of these perfectly ordinary events to ghosts.

The second part of the problem concerns Mrs. Garrett's alleged contact with the spirit of Andreas, the soldier who was supposed to have died in the house. As stated, the house probably did figure somehow in the Revolutionary War. This fact was well known to everyone who attended the séance, including the medium. Perhaps a Polish soldier named Andreas was beaten to death in that house. But there is not a shred of confirming evidence that this happened.

A search of the records of the army of the time turned up several soldiers named Andreas, who might have been the man, but none of them seemed to fill the bill. This utter lack of confirming evidence does not immediately prove that the story as related in the séance never happened. Records of the time are incomplete, and in the whole panorama of the Revolutionary War, the brutal death of a single ordinary soldier, particularly one without a family in America, may easily have gone unrecorded, or the records may since have been lost. But without any confirming evidence we simply have to take the medium's word for what happened. We are confronted with the same problems concerning the reliability of mediums that have confronted psychical researchers since they began their search for ghosts nearly a century ago.

A lot of what passes for the investigation of haunted houses today involves the use of mediums. A self-styled "ghost hunter" or "psychical researcher" will bring a medium to a house that is supposed to be haunted. The medium will go into a trance, and say that she is in contact with this or that spirit, that had once lived, and died in the house. This can make an enjoyable spooky story, and a believable one, if you are a spiritualist who is convinced that mediums are in contact with the dead. But not even all mediums are convinced of this. Remember, Mrs. Piper wondered whether she was "possessed or obsessed." Mrs. Garrett finally came to the conclusion that Unvani and the other "spirits" that spoke through her were not spirits at all but some parts of her own unconscious personality.

Not all investigations of haunted houses involve using a medium. Let's look at another fairly typical modern haunting. This one took place in Yorkshire, England, in 1953, and is known as the York Museum ghost. The haunting began on September 20.

The day was Sunday, and the museum was being used for a small meeting. The meeting ended after seven and the museum's caretaker, George L. Jonas, was getting ready to lock up when he heard footsteps coming from the floor above. At first he thought the steps were being made by a member of the museum's staff who was working late. He went upstairs to tell the staff member that he was ready to close up and go home. But the man upstairs wasn't anybody that Jonas had ever seen before.

"I thought he was an odd looking chap, because he was wearing a frock-coat, drain pipe trousers, and had fluffy side whiskers. He had very little hair and walked with a slight stoop.

"I decided he might be an eccentric professor. As I neared the top of the stairs, he seemed to change his mind, turn and walk back into the office. When I got to the door, he seemed to change his mind again and turned quickly to come out."

Jonas tried to speak to the figure but the old man didn't answer and apparently didn't hear him. The figure headed for the library.

"Being only a few feet from him, I saw his face clearly and could pick him out from a photograph any time. He looked agitated, had a frown on his face, and kept muttering; 'I must find it; I must find it.'

"It was queer, but I did not think about ghosts for one minute. He looked just as real as you or me. But I did not want him roaming around so late at night, and anyway I wanted to lock up and catch my bus."

The oddly dressed figure went into the library where Jonas caught up with him. "He was standing between two tall book racks pulling first one book and then another from one of the

The ruins of Borley Rectory in April, 1944. Borley Rectory had the reputation of being "the most haunted house in England." However, a great controversy has surrounded the alleged hauntings and some prominent psychical researchers have charged that most of the phenomena were faked. White spot in lower righthand corner is supposed to be a brick poised in mid-air against the black background of the passage entrance.

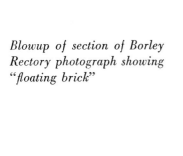

*Blowup of section of Borley
Rectory photograph showing
"floating brick"*

shelves. He seemed anxious to find something.

"I thought to myself, this has gone far enough. So, thinking he was deaf, I stretched my right hand out to touch him on the shoulder. But as my hand drew near his coat he vanished, and the book he had been holding dropped to the floor."

Jonas reported what he had seen to another member of the museum staff. For several Sundays the two of them waited for the ghostly figure to appear again. But nothing happened for three weeks. Then on Sunday, October 18, the figure did appear at exactly the same time that it had first been seen. But by that time the caretaker's companion, who had already spent three fruitless Sunday evenings waiting for the ghost, had already gone home. The figure came down the stairs and passed through the closed library door. Jonas did not attempt to follow it.

In November another man joined Jonas in his hunt for the ghost. On Sunday, November 15, as the men awaited the arrival of the ghost, Jonas said he had a "feeling" it was already in the library. The library door was unlocked, and the two men advanced cautiously into it. Jonas went down one side of the room while his companion went down another. There was a dull thud, and both men rushed to the shelf at which the ghost had been seen before. They found a book lying on the floor. The pages were still fluttering as though it had just been dropped.

This series of unsettling experiences put the caretaker, who was known as an emotional man anyway, in a highly nervous state. Jonas' doctor was skeptical about the ghost, but worried about his patient. Jonas, however, insisted time after time that he was not "seeing things." He had figured out that the ghost appeared every fourth Sunday at almost exactly 7:40 P.M. Since the ghost visited on such a regular schedule, Jonas asked his doctor if he would be part of a group that was going to be in the York Museum library at the time of the ghost's next scheduled arrival, Sunday, December 13. Reluctantly the doctor agreed.

On that date the caretaker, his doctor, a lawyer, and a number of people connected with the museum gathered in the library at about 7 P.M. They seated themselves around the bookshelf where the ghostly browser had seemed to have been seeking a particular volume. The group of observers were watching the shelves, and one another, to make sure that no trickery took place.

At almost precisely 7:40 P.M. a book popped out of the shelf and landed on the floor. Said the doctor: "I was immediately at the spot. The book was lying with the leaves still moving, about one inch from the bookcase facing the latter. An immediate inspection of the shelf showed that there was nothing there, and neither was there anything on the other side of the bookcase, the bookcase being one with an aisle on each side. An inspection with a torch produced nothing further. There was no physical means [of] making the book move." The name of the book was *Antiquities and Curiosities of the Church,* published in 1896.

The doctor told newspaper reporters later, "It's absolutely incredible. Without a doubt that book was taken from the shelf by something not of this world."

The lawyer added, "I wouldn't have acted for anybody who told me a story like this, but we have the proof with our own eyes."

Said Jonas, "Maybe now someone will believe me." A lot of people believed him.

A scholarly ghost whose only action is to take a book out of a shelf and drop it on the floor is a far cry from the fearsome chain-rattling spectres of yesteryear. But this case is quite typical of a modern ghost story. Nothing violent happened, yet the events are quite eerie. Newspapers all over the world picked up the story. People from countries as far away as India and Argentina had read of the York Museum ghost. Here is a fairly restrained account of the events that appeared in an English newspaper:

"The ghost in Edwardian dress is haunting the York Museum. Eight reliable citizens, including a doctor and a solicitor, watched in frozen silence as an unseen hand slowly drew a book from a shelf in the library and dropped it at their feet.

"The Thing has been coming every fourth Sunday at exactly the same time since it was first seen by the museum's caretaker, Mr. George Jonas."

147

Naturally the Society for Psychical Research heard about the York Museum ghost, and sought to investigate it. There was some trouble and confusion about making arrangements to visit the museum. It was not until Sunday, February 7, two four-week periods after the startling events of December 13, that a group of experienced psychical researchers were able to set up watch in the library of the York Museum. They practically had to fight off a horde of newspaper reporters to do it. Finally, after a good deal of hard arguing, the reporters agreed to wait outside the museum until the investigation was finished.

The appointed time for the ghost's arrival came and went, but nothing happened. Jonas said that he thought he had seen a ghostly hand reaching for a book, but no one else saw it. The investigators left the museum and explained to the disappointed reporters, that they had nothing at all to report. The ghost, if there ever had been one, had not put in an appearance that night. And that was the end of the story of the York Museum ghost as far as the press was concerned.

But it was not the end of the investigation for the psychical researchers. Naturally they suspected a hoax. One of the investigators, Trevor H. Hall, knew a good deal about conjuring and stage magic. He knew that one of the magician's most effective tools is a plain black thread. In a fairly dark room—and the light was poor in the York Museum library—such a thread is virtually invisible.

In his own library, Hall devised a simple method by which a thread could be attached to a shelf, and looped around the back of a particular book. Then it would take just a slight pull on the thread to make the book jump out of the shelf. It looked just as if an unseen hand had pulled the book from the shelf. The people seated around the bookshelf would probably not have noticed that one of their number had pulled a thread. The necessary motion would be too slight, and they would have been more intent on watching the bookshelf. In the confusion that followed the book's fall the thread could have been overlooked, or pocketed by the hoaxer.

The researchers concluded that the book that had fallen out of the shelf in front of witnesses had not been pulled out by any ghostly hand, but rather by a simple black thread.

Oddly enough, however, the researchers also decided that the entire story was not the result of a deliberate hoax and that the caretaker had really seen a ghost, or rather thought that he had. They said that he probably suffered a real hallucination and had become very worried about it. That is why he asked others to share his experience. He wanted them to believe him. Naturally they could not share his hallucination.

Hall, and another investigator, Eric J. Dingwall, explained their conclusions this way. "If, for instance, we are told that Mr. X has had a vivid dream of being presented with a gold medal, we shall see no good reason for disbelieving it if we know enough of Mr. X to credit his story at all. But if we are told the gold medal was found in the bed when Mr. X woke up in the morning we should be inclined to suggest a normal explanation for such a strange occurrence. The reason is that, so far as we know, dreams do not work like that and neither do apparitions —which, after all, are merely hallucinations of another kind."

They concluded, "We know little enough of dreams and apparitions as it is, but that is no reason why we should accept stories of events which seem clearly to violate the few rules we do know."

Thus in the view of these psychical researchers the whole affair started with a genuine hallucination. The caretaker had no reason to make up a story about a ghost, and a lot of reasons not to. Perhaps while prowling about the library in search of the ghost a book was accidentally dislodged from the shelf. Under the circumstances he could easily have been frightened enough to assume that the ghost had pulled the book from the shelf. Trickery may only have entered the case of the York Museum ghost at the end. Who was the trickster? The caretaker or someone else who simply wanted to keep the exciting story alive? The researchers do not say.

There are no really clear distinctions between a house that is supposed to be haunted, and one that is supposed to be infested by a poltergeist, except that poltergeists are generally heard and not seen. Another feature of poltergeists is that the manifestations seem rather purposeless, and usually center about a young person, or take place only when a particular young person is present. Poltergeists are probably the most common of all the strange occurrences investigated by psychical researchers.

A typical case took place in 1958. The site of this poltergeist or haunting was not a crumbling castle or deserted mansion in Europe. It was a very ordinary ranch-style home in the very ordinary suburban community of Seaford, Long Island. Like most poltergeists, the Seaford poltergeist indulged mainly in producing loud unexplainable noises, and occasionally throwing objects about. This particular poltergeist seemed to have a great fondness for popping the tops of bottles, or unscrewing screw-top lids and spilling the contents of the bottle.

The afflicted house was owned by the Hermann family. They had two children—a girl Lucille, thirteen, and a boy Jimmy, twelve. The phenomena seemed to center about the boy. He was either the sole witness, or quite nearby when most strange things happened.

The Hermann family was very upset by the goings on in their house. They openly appealed for help. For that reason the case got an enormous amount of publicity. It may well have been the most well-publicized "haunting" of the twentieth century.

Among those who were attracted by the case was Dr. J. G. Pratt, than a member of the faculty of Duke University. Dr. Pratt was an associate of Dr. J. B. Rhine, America's leading researcher in the field of "paranormal" phenomena, which includes hauntings and poltergeists.

Dr. Pratt came to the Long Island house to investigate. He carefully interviewed everyone who had seen or heard anything unusual. He checked the house and all the objects in it carefully to make sure that there could be no natural explanation for the various phenomena. The poltergeist had quieted down considerably by the time Dr. Pratt arrived, but he did hear some strange thumps coming from Jimmy's room. When he had finished his investigation, Dr. Pratt was just about as puzzled as when he had started. "We reached no conclusions regarding the case itself," he wrote.

However, in New York City a magician named Milbourne Christopher had some pretty good ideas about the causes of the strange phenomena. Christopher was head of the Occult Investigation Committee of the Society of American Magicians, and had already conducted similar investigations. He phoned the Hermann house and asked permission to visit and conduct his own investigation. Mr. Hermann turned him down. He said he didn't want any "charlatans, mystics, mediums, or magicians" in his house.

Dr. Pratt accepted an invitation to visit Christopher's home in New York, after he had completed his work at Seaford. "As we talked about poltergeists," wrote Christopher, "a china figurine leapt from a bookcase shelf and landed some eight feet away by a television set." It was a trick, of course, but Dr. Pratt was unable to figure out how the magician had done it.

Christopher stated that he could reproduce all the phenomena that had taken place in the Seaford house. He demonstrated this for several groups of reporters. One story of a demonstration began:

"Milbourne Christopher sat back in an easy chair, offered a wave of his hand and said that the house in Seaford, Long Island, was no more haunted than his place. Just then the tops of several bottles unscrewed themselves in the bathroom, and an object went flying from a pile of magazines to the floor several feet away."

Dr. Pratt had naturally considered the idea of trickery in the Seaford case, but he rejected it. He was not impressed by the magician's demonstrations. He contended that while a skilled magician might be able to reproduce most of the phenomena, no one in the Seaford house was a skilled magician, and thus trickery was impossible.

Christopher countered by saying that the talents of a skilled magician were entirely unnecessary, and that the phenomena were very easy to reproduce. How had he managed to unscrew bottle caps in one room while seated in another? Simple. He unscrewed the bottle caps before the reporters arrived, and then with the reporters present made a noise that sounded like popping bottle caps. He just rapped his knuckles on a doorframe then immediately turned his head toward the bathroom, as if the sound had come from that direction. When the reporters found the bottle caps unscrewed they simply assumed that the noise and the bottles were connected.

Wrote Christopher, "Hearing is the easiest of the five senses to deceive. A simple test you can try is this: Have someone sit in a chair with his eyes closed. Walk around the chair, then reach over his head and click two coins together. Ask him to point immediately in the direction of the sound. You'll be intrigued with the result."

The flying objects were made to fly with the aid of the magician's old friend—the black thread. A black thread could also have been used to make the objects in the Seaford house fly about.

Some of the phenomena reported in the Seaford house could not have been produced by simple tricks. But were these particular events reported exactly as they happened? The members of the family were under a great deal of stress, and under such conditions witnesses often do not report events exactly as they happened, but rather they report what they think happened. Under the calmest of conditions most people are very poor witnesses anyway. And certainly people who suspect that they are living in a haunted house are not going to feel particularly calm.

Many psychical researchers would have tended to agree with Christopher rather than Dr. Pratt. Historically, poltergeists and trickery have gone together. Often the tricksters are young people who are bored, unhappy, angry, or simply want attention. Parents often refuse to believe that they could be fooled, or that their own children could play such tricks. In this sort of an atmosphere simple tricks can create an enormous amount of excitement in a household. Recall that the Fox sisters confessed that they had started the whole spiritualism movement by dropping apples on the floor and cracking their toe joints.

The British psychical researcher D. J. West has written, "Until investigators can themselves witness the extraordinary antics of the poltergeist, and can see and photograph the objects while they are actually jumping about of their own accord, the only

Hannath Hall in Cambridgeshire, England, where poltergeist activity has frequently been reported during recent years

reasonable attitude is one of severe skepticism."

Not all poltergeist cases, however, fall under suspicion of trickery. An unusual case was investigated in England in 1955 by Trevor H. Hall, one of the men who had helped to track the ghost of the York Museum. This poltergeist was attacking a house in the town of Ousedale that was being used as a doctors' office. The disturbances consisted mostly of very loud, and unexplained noises, though on one or two occasions objects were seen to move around. What made this case particularly interesting is that neither the doctors, nor any of their staff put much faith in supernatural explanations for the noises at first. So they were not inclined to exaggerate the evidence.

154

When the noises began, the doctors did the usual thing. First they called in the plumber to check the pipes. Then the gas and the electricity men were called in, and finally the police. Everything in the house seemed perfectly normal, and no one could come up with an explanation for the noises. Only then did the doctors begin to wonder whether their house might be haunted. Finally one of the doctors contacted Hall.

Hall interviewed all the witnesses and decided to pretty much rule out the idea of trickery from the start. There were no children in the house and it is usually children who fake poltergeists. None of those Hall interviewed seemed to possess the personality of a prankster. Besides, the noises occasionally occurred when all those who could possibly have faked them were in the same room together.

Since the gas, water, and electricity had already been eliminated as a source of the noises, Hall thought the house itself might be the cause. The house did seem "disturbed." The plaster on the inside was cracked in many places, and the doors and windows had shifted badly out of line. This had not happened because the house was poorly constructed. The problem was that the ground underneath the house was unstable. As the house shifted, the plaster cracked and the window and door frames bent. Hall knew of several cases where shifting ground has caused loud noises inside a house. "Anyone who has had experience in mining areas knows that loud and disturbing noises can be produced by the movement of a house standing on land which is subsiding."

Two problems remained. First, the noises only occurred at certain times, and there seemed to be a sort of pattern to them. What was the reason for this pattern? Second, if the ground in the area was shifting why was only this house affected?

Hall suspected that the key to both of these problems was underground water. The house itself stood fairly near the mouth of the river Ouse. The river at Ousedale rose and fell with the tides. By checking a table of tides Hall found that the times of the highest tides in Ousedale coincided perfectly with the times of the loudest noises in the house. He theorized that there might be an old sewer running under the house and down to the river. If the sewer under the house had become blocked, then the water at highest tide might back up in it, and put considerable stress on the foundations of the house. This would cause the house to shift slightly, and create the noises.

No real search for an underground sewer was ever undertaken because that would have involved a lot of digging, and psychical researchers rarely have enough time or money for such extensive projects. So you might say that the cause of the strange noises in the house at Ousedale was not proved conclusively. But the weight of evidence favoring underground water, rather than ghosts, is overwhelming.

This, then, is a fairly representative selection of poltergeists and modern hauntings. Of course, more sensational sounding cases appear in newspapers, magazines, and books all of the time. But it is well to remember that the York Museum ghost and the Seaford poltergeist sounded pretty sensational too, when they were first reported in the press.

8

Apparitions and Spirit Photographs

One of the best real ghost stories of modern times took place at the end of the First World War.

Lieutenant David McConnell was an eighteen-year-old British trainee pilot. On the morning of December 7, 1918, his commanding officer unexpectedly asked him to fly a small plane to a field at Tadcaster, some sixty miles from his home base at Scampton. Another pilot was to accompany him in a two-seater plane. McConnell was to leave his plane at Tadcaster. It was to be the second pilot's job to bring McConnell back to his home base as soon as he had completed his mission.

At 11:30 A.M. McConnell told his roommate, Lieutenant Larkin, that he had to deliver an airplane to Tadcaster, but that he expected to be back that same afternoon.

The sixty-mile flight from Scampton to Tadcaster was a routine one under normal conditions. But along the way the two pilots ran into a heavy fog. They landed and telephoned their home base for instructions. McConnell was told to use his own discretion, so they took off again for Tadcaster. The fog got thicker and McConnell's companion in the two-seater made a forced landing. McConnell, however, continued the flight to Tad-

157

caster. Upon reaching the field he started his approach for landing at a bad angle and crashed. McConnell was thrown violently
forward and smashed his head on the gun mounted in front of
him. A witness to the crash rushed to the plane and found the
pilot dead. His watch had been broken in the crash and was
stopped at exactly 3:25 P.M.

At the same time that McConnell crashed at Tadcaster his
roommate Larkin was sitting in their room at Scampton reading
and smoking. He heard footsteps coming up the corridor and
heard the door behind him open. Then he heard the familiar
words, "Hello boy!" This was McConnell's customary greeting.
Larkin turned around and saw McConnell—or what looked like
McConnell— standing in the doorway, about eight feet behind
him. He was dressed in the standard flying outfit, but instead of
a flying helmet he was wearing a naval cap. McConnell often
wore a naval cap because he had served in the Naval Air Service
and was very proud of that.

To Larkin there seemed nothing odd about McConnell's coming in at that moment. He said, "Hello! Back already?" The
figure replied, "Yes. Got there all right. Had a good trip." The
figure then said, "Well, cheerio!" and went out, closing the door
behind him.

A little while later—the time was a quarter to four—another
officer, Lieutenant Garner Smith, came into the room. Garner
Smith said that he hoped that McConnell would be back early
so that the three of them could go out that evening. Larkin said
that McConnell was already back, and that he had been in the
room, less than half an hour ago. Thus, McConnell, or something that looked like McConnell, had appeared to Larkin between 3:15 and 3:30. McConnell, we know, was killed at 3:25.

Larkin didn't even hear of his roommate's death until that

evening. At first he assumed that McConnell had returned at about three in the afternoon, come to the room, and then gone out on another flight during which he was killed. Only hours later did Larkin realize that McConnell had been killed at almost exactly the same moment that he had seen McConnell standing in the door, and had talked to him. The next morning Larkin related the incident to other officers on the base. Garner Smith confirmed his part of the story.

Despite what he saw, Larkin remained skeptical about ghosts, and other psychical matters. But he had no other explanation to offer. This strange story got around the base, and when McConnell's family came to claim his body they heard of it and wrote to Larkin immediately. He replied on December 22 and set down a clear, matter of fact account of the incident.

Eventually the McConnell case came to the attention of the Society for Psychical Research, which maintains an extensive file on such experiences. Though it happened over sixty years ago, the McConnell case is still generally considered one of the best, if not *the* best story of its type in the S.P.R. files.

While the McConnell case is good, it is not unique. There have been many similar experiences recorded. In fact, the tale of the image of a person who had just died, or is about to die, appearing to a friend or relative some distance away is remarkably common. Why is this case considered particularly good? A look at the reasons will tell us something about what constitutes good evidence for a scrupulous psychical researcher.

In the first place, the witness to the apparition seems to have been a reliable, level-headed individual, not the sort likely to make up stories, or who habitually "sees things."

Secondly, the witness wrote down his version of the event just two weeks after it took place. You will recall the case of Sir

Trick photograph showing a frightening "ghost"

Edmund Hornby who saw the reporter's ghost in his room. Sir Edmund was also a reliable witness, but he did not write down his account until some nine years after the event. In that time memory can play all sorts of strange tricks. It would have been better if Larkin had written down his experience immediately after hearing of McConnell's death, for the details would have been fresher in his mind. But Larkin certainly did not know at the time that his experience would become a psychical classic.

He may not have cared very much either. Larkin did tell his story to others the day after McConnell's death. Those who heard the story said the written report conformed to what they had been told.

Another thing that makes this case most impressive is that there was a confirming witness—not to the reality of the apparition itself, but to Larkin's belief that he had seen his roommate, when in reality the man was dead many miles away. All the times seem well established. The time of McConnell's death was established most dramatically by his smashed wrist watch. Larkin could not possibly have known of McConnell's death at the time he told Garner Smith that he had just seen McConnell.

Did McConnell's ghost appear to his roommate at the moment of his death? If it did not, what did happen?

First we must consider the possibility of a hoax. There is, of course, no material evidence of the apparition. Larkin may simply have made up the story and Garner Smith may have been in on the hoax. It may seem strange to propose that two British Air Force officers would concoct a hoax concerning the death of a friend. It isn't the sort of thing that men treat lightly. The only reason for hoaxing that seems to make any sense in this case is that the two officers invented the story to comfort McConnell's parents. But Larkin never sought out McConnell's parents to tell them what he had seen. They seem to have heard of the apparition almost by accident. Thus the possibility of a hoax is remote, but it must be kept in mind.

What about mistaken identification? This has proved to be the solution of many cases of this type. Apparitions are usually vague and indistinct figures that are glimpsed only briefly. Under such conditions mistakes are easy to make. But in this case the witness not only looked at the apparition for a considerable period of time, he also spoke to it, heard its footsteps, and heard it open and shut the door. Larkin was absolutely convinced he had seen a solid, living man.

Perhaps another pilot entered the room and Larkin mistakenly assumed that he was McConnell. The conversation between the two was brief, and McConnell's name was never mentioned. The pilots were mostly young men who looked pretty much alike in their flying suits. But McConnell wore a very distinct naval cap, and this probably rules out a mistake of that kind.

Larkin may have dreamed the entire incident. Perhaps he dozed off in his chair while reading. In his sleep he heard the noise of someone coming down the hall. He then simply incorporated that noise into his dream, and dreamed of the arrival of his roommate whom he had been expecting. Dreams sometimes do work that way. In sleep experiments psychologists have shown that if a bell is rung, sometimes a sleeper will dream of a fire engine, or if a bit of water is sprinkled on a sleeper he may dream he is standing in the rain. To be dreaming of someone at the exact moment that the person is killed is a rather remarkable coincidence in itself. But remarkable coincidences do sometimes happen, and they do not necessarily require a supernatural explanation.

Yet Larkin insisted that he wasn't asleep. He said that he was not only reading but smoking at the time, and it would have been impossible for him to fall asleep without burning himself. He certainly was not asleep when Garner Smith entered the room. So to the idea that he dreamed he saw McConnell we must conclude—possible, but unlikely.

Could the figure of the dead pilot have been a hallucination? Here we get into a pretty confusing area. Some psychical researchers think that hallucinations are merely waking dreams, while others insist that hallucinations, apparitions, and ghosts are all pretty much the same thing. They theorize that McConnell's death released some sort of "psychic energy," and that this created the hallucination or apparition in the mind of his friend who may have been thinking about him at that moment. Most scientists would disagree with this theory because there has never been any concrete evidence of any sort of "psychic energy." In fact, no one really knows what hallucinations—or dreams, for that matter—really are or how they are produced.

The McConnell case remains as puzzling and intriguing as when it first went into the files of the S.P.R.

We can't really come to any grand conclusions about apparitions and ghosts on the basis of a single case, no matter how strange it may appear. Way back in 1890 the S.P.R. had heard enough cases like this to wonder how common they might really be. They asked several thousand people in England this question:

"Have you ever, when believing yourself to be completely awake, had a vivid impression of seeing or being touched by a living being or inanimate object, or of hearing a voice, which impression, so far as you could distinguish, was not due to any external physical cause?"

The investigators reported that some 10 per cent of the people they questioned had, or believed they had, such an experience. A half century later a similar survey was conducted. This time 14 per cent said they had an experience that might be classed as a hallucination. So it seems that hallucinations—whatever they may be—are more common than most people think. And a person doesn't have to be crazy, drunk, drugged, or in any other abnormal mental state to have a hallucination.

The S.P.R. investigators also found a fairly large number of cases in which people said that they saw an apparition of a person within twelve hours of the death of that person. This seemed highly significant. While hallucinations themselves might be "normal," even common, the number of hallucinations connected with the death of a person seemed to imply something quite beyond the ordinary. The investigators did admit that some of these cases might be the result of coincidence, bad reporting, faulty memory, or just plain lies. Skeptics who have examined the very same evidence say all of the cases could easily fall into one of these categories, and that there is no need to bring in psychic impressions, ghosts, or anything out of the ordinary to explain them.

None of the cases collected in 1890 was anywhere near as impressive as the McConnell case. Nor have any collected since that time surpassed the McConnell case in the quality of evidence. While many startling sounding cases like this are publicized every year in books, magazines, and newspapers, very few have been investigated closely. Usually the writer is more interested in getting a good story than in getting the facts of the case. Facts sometimes get in the way of a good story.

So there we are again—the case is fascinating but not conclusive.

In order to find something more solid than stories which may or may not be true and accurate, many people have attempted to photograph ghosts. The result has not always been a happy one.

Spiritualism and photography became popular at about the same time. Spirit photographs of one sort or another were already being produced back in the 1860's. The first well-known instance of "spirit" photography took place in Boston in 1862. A professional photographer named Mumler said that he had taken his own self-portrait. When he developed the picture he

Charles Foster and an affectionate "spirit." One of the earliest "spirit" photographs taken.

found that it also contained the image of a cousin who had been dead for twelve years.

When the news of this marvel got around in spiritualist circles the spiritualists flocked to Mumler to have their pictures taken with dead friends and relatives. Mumler began turning out spirit photographs by the bushel. Most of the "spirits" in these photographs were heavily draped and in such poor focus that it was almost impossible to make out any features clearly. Yet many of those who got photographs from Mumler unhesitatingly identified the indistinct figures as being the image of dead friends and relatives. Some of Mumler's spirit photographs must have been a little too clear, however, because the "spirits" in them were recognized as living people who also happened to work for the photographer. Mumler left Boston in a hurry, but he turned up a few years later doing exactly the same thing in New York City. The city tried to prosecute Mumler for fraud, but numerous witnesses appeared who said that he was not a faker because he had provided them with photographs of their dead loved ones. The charges against the photographer were dismissed.

Most spirit photographs were remarkably easy to produce. The photographer took a picture of the subject who wished to receive a "spirit photograph." He then took another picture on the same piece of film of the "spirit," usually a heavily draped assistant, though some "spirit" photographers cut costs by using dummies. Thus the spirit photographs were simply double exposures.

Some "spirit" photographers employed even cruder methods. They simply cut out faces of famous people and superimposed them on a photograph that they had taken. Occasionally they painted in some swirls of clouds around the floating face to make

How "spirit" photographs were made. Photographer's accomplice dressed as a spirit might sneak in behind the subject being photographed.

it look more "spiritual" and to hide the sharp outlines of the cutouts. There are scores of "spirit photographs" that contain the face of Abraham Lincoln.

Most of the spirit photographs that were produced during this period were so obviously faked that it is hard to imagine how anyone was foolish enough to take them seriously. But a lot of people did take them seriously, and some people still do. People often believe what they want to believe, no matter how strongly their beliefs are refuted by the evidence.

Take the case of a French "spirit" photographer named Buget, who operated in London and Paris during the 1870's. Buget did a booming business and his photographs were endorsed as genuine by many of the leading spiritualists of the time.

At first Buget used his assistants to pose as the spirits. But as his business grew he began to worry that the repetition of the same few faces time after time might be noticed even by the spiritualists. So he switched from living models for spirits to using a dummy with a large number of interchangeable heads. The assistants would ask a sitter what spirit he wished to get a picture of, and Buget would choose a proper head accordingly. Sometimes Buget would be able to obtain a picture of the person whose "spirit" he was to photograph. Thus he could make his dummy appear more true to life.

In 1875 Buget was arrested by the French government for selling fraudulent photographs. The police seized the "spirit" dummy and all its extra heads. Buget himself made a full confession to the charge of faking photographs. But at his trial an amazing thing happened. Witness after witness stepped forward to proclaim that the photograph that he had received could not possibly have been faked. Many refused to believe Buget's own confession, and rejected the evidence of the dummy and the photographer's other trick apparatus that was on display in the courtroom.

Here is a bit of typical testimony from the trial. The witness was a man named Dessenon, a picture seller aged fifty-five. He explained that he had first received several spirit photographs which he had not recognized, but then:

"The portrait of my wife, which I had specially asked for, is so like her that when I showed it to one of my relatives he exclaimed, 'It's my cousin.'

THE COURT. Was that chance, Buget?

BUGET. Yes, pure chance. I had no photograph of Madame Dessenon.

THE WITNESS. My children, like myself, thought the likeness perfect. When I showed them the picture, they cried, 'It's mamma.'

THE COURT. You see this doll and all the rest of the things?

THE WITNESS. There is nothing there in the least like the photograph which I obtained.

THE COURT. You may stand down.

The spiritualists naturally refused to admit that they had been taken in by a faker. They asserted that Buget was a genuine medium, and said that he had been bribed or terrorized into making a false confession and fabricating the dummy and all the other apparatus for making fake photographs in order to discredit spiritualism.

Despite the spiritualists' strong and persistent defense of Buget, the trial did tend to put "spirit" photography in a bad light. This type of "spirit" photography continued to be practiced, and it is still practiced on a small scale today. But it is not taken seriously by many people anymore.

Other types of "spirit photographs," however, deserve a little closer attention. During the late nineteenth and early twentieth centuries some photographers, who had no intention of producing phony "spirit photographs," would develop their pictures and find a faint and ghostly image in the scene, when none should have been there. Occasionally such an indistinct figure would be identified as being someone who had recently died.

In the early 1900's an English photographer was taking a picture of the inside of a chapel. When he developed the photograph he observed a faintly discernible human face in one of the panels. He recognized the face as that of a young friend who had recently died a tragic death. The photographer showed the photograph to psychical researcher Frank Podmore. Podmore

169

*A medium supposedly sur-
rounded by her materialized
spirit controls*

was one of the most skeptical of the early psychical researchers.
He thoroughly disbelieved spiritualist claims, and thought that
"spirit" photography was nonsense. Yet, said Podmore, "When
he told me the story and showed me the picture, I could easily
see the faint but well-marked features of a handsome, melan-
choly lad of eighteen."

Podmore then took the photograph and showed it to another
friend of his, but did not tell him the story about the boy who
had died. Podmore's friend at once identified the face in the
photograph as belonging to a woman of about thirty. Podmore
commented, "The outlines are in reality so indistinct as to leave
ample room for the imagination to work in."

How had this "spirit photograph" been produced in the first place? The answer to this question lay in the way that photographs were taken many years ago. The film of the time was crude and slow compared to the film we use today, and it took a long time to take a photograph. In a place where the light was not very good—and this particular photograph was taken inside a chapel—the film might have to be exposed for an hour or more. The photographer usually set up his camera on a tripod, and then just walked away from it. If during that period someone walked into the scene that was being photographed and paused for a few seconds to look at the camera, that person's face and figure would register in a faint and ghostly way on the film. If the photographer did not know that someone had gone into the room he might be inclined to believe that he had photographed a ghost.

Today we have much faster films, and photographs are made in fractions of a second. Mistakes like this cannot happen. But even today there are a few "spirit photographs" produced every year. Most of these photographs do not show a human figure at all, but rather a blur or strange light that is assumed, by the photographer, to be a ghost. Occasionally such photographs are faked, but more often they are the result of honest mistakes. If there is something wrong with the camera or film, or some error in the developing process takes place, photographs may turn out with strange lights or blurs on them. If you owned a camera that regularly produced pictures with strange streaks and blurs on them you might, if you were so inclined, assume you were taking "spirit photographs." You would be more likely to take it to a camera shop and see if it could be repaired.

The magician James Randi once told the author of an experience that he had with a "spirit" photographer. He had heard of

APPARITIONS AND SPIRIT PHOTOGRAPHS

John H. Cutten, honorary secretary of the British Society for Psychical Research, made these two "spirit" photographs, to show how easily such pictures can be produced. Photograph above shows a "ghostly couple" in cloisters. Photograph below shows a "ghost" rising from the grave of poet W. B. Yeats.

a little old lady who regularly took "spirit photographs" of her friends. The "spirits" in these pictures were just irregular blobs and streaks of light. Randi asked to see the camera used to take the photographs, and the lady was delighted to show it to him.

The camera was an old-fashioned bellows type. Randi noticed at once that the bellows was cracked and split in places. Light seeped in through these cracks and produced the "spirits" in the photographs. The old lady, however, had not known there was anything wrong with the camera. Randi took some tape and repaired the cracks in the bellows and gave the camera back to her.

A few days later he called her to ask how the camera was working. She burst into tears when she heard his voice and refused to speak to him. From other sources he heard that the woman had tried to use her camera after Randi repaired it and was heartbroken to discover that she was no longer able to obtain "spirit photographs." She was sure that somehow Randi's impure touch had destroyed whatever psychic powers the camera had possessed.

But the story has a happy ending, at least for the old lady. She shopped around in secondhand camera stores until she found another old camera that would take the same sort of "spirit photographs." She didn't know that there was anything wrong with this camera either. It seemed just as "good" as the camera she used to have before Randi "ruined" it. At last report she was happily taking "spirit photographs" once again.

A Selected Bibliography

There are hundreds of books on ghosts and psychical research in general. More and more of them appear every year. But this huge mass of material has to be viewed with a highly critical eye. Books of "true" experiences with ghosts, written by people who call themselves "ghost hunters" or even "psychical researchers," usually are not true at all. They are just highly imaginative accounts of strange experiences. Often such books are a lot of fun to read, but they should not be regarded as serious research. The same must be said for many of the other popular books written on psychic subjects. After all, anyone can call himself a "psychical researcher." Many people who write such books also like to label themselves hardheaded and skeptical journalists. Journalists they may be; they may also be hardheaded and skeptical, in private, but their books are written for the benefit of a credulous and sensation hungry public.

Listed below are a group of books, either entirely about ghosts and the history of psychical research, or which bear heavily on these subjects. The attitudes of the authors range from extreme skepticism, to total belief, and all shades in between. However, the books can be recommended as honest attempts to present the subjects, rather than attempts to exploit and sensationalize them.

Brown, Slater. *The Heyday of Spiritualism.* New York: Hawthorn Books, 1970.

174

A history of nineteenth-century spiritualism, particularly in America. The writer professes to believe almost all the claims, but he tells his story accurately and well.

Christopher, Milbourne. *ESP, Seers and Psychics: What the Occult Is.* New York: Thomas Y. Crowell Co., 1970.
A leading magician's experiences with opinions on modern occultism.

_____. *Houdini, the Untold Story.* New York: Thomas Y. Crowell Co., 1969.
Contains an excellent account of Arthur Ford and the "Houdini code" incident.

Cohen, Daniel. *Masters of the Occult.* New York: Dodd, Mead & Company, 1971.
Contains brief biographies of some famous mediums.

_____. *Myths of the Space Age.* New York: Dodd, Mead & Company, 1967.
This book is subtitled "A skeptic's inquiry into the pseudo-scientific world of today."

_____. *Superstition.* Mankato, Minnesota: Creative Education Press, 1971.
A look at odd beliefs and the reasons behind them. Written for young people aged ten and up. Many illustrations.

De Camp, L. Sprague and Catherine. *Spirits, Stars, and Spells.* New York: Canaveral Press, 1966.
A highly skeptical, and very lively account of spiritualism, witchcraft, magic and a lot of other strange things.

Dingwall, Eric J. *Some Human Oddities.* London: Home and Van Thal, 1947.
Among the oddities is the famed medium D. D. Home.

Dingwall, Eric J., Goldney, K. M., and Hall, Trevor H. *The Haunting of Borley Rectory.* London: Gerald Duckworth and Co., 1955.
A classic exposé of "the most haunted house in all England."

Dingwall, Eric J. and Hall, Trevor H. *Four Modern Ghosts*. London: Gerald Duckworth and Co., 1958.

Includes complete accounts of the York Museum ghost and the Ousedale Haunt.

Garrett, Eileen J. *Many Voices*. New York: G. P. Putnam's Sons, 1968.

The autobiography of a famed medium. Perhaps the most intelligent book ever written by a professional psychic.

Hall, Trevor H. *New Light on Old Ghosts*. London: Gerald Duckworth and Co., 1965.

_____. *The Spiritualists*. New York: Helix Press, Garrett Publications, 1963.

This book and the one above re-examine some celebrated cases of psychical research in a highly unfavorable light.

Hansel, C.E.M. *ESP: A Scientific Evaluation*. New York: Charles Scribners Sons, 1966.

This book established its author as the world's leading scientific critic of all psychical research. It is a classic.

Houdini, Harry. *Houdini on Magic*. New York: Dover Publications, 1963.

Houdini explains some of the tricks used by Margery and other mediums.

Houdini, Harry and Dunninger, J. *Houdini's Spirit World, Dunninger's Psychic Revelations*. New York: Tower Publications, 1970.

A collection of articles on spiritualism and other psychic phenomena by the two magicians.

Jastrow, Joseph. *Error and Eccentricity*. New York: Dover Publications, 1962.

A psychologist examines human credulity.

Kettlekamp, Larry. *Haunted Houses*. New York: William Morrow, 1969.

A book for young readers on some famous haunts. The author believes in ghosts.

A SELECTED BIBLIOGRAPHY

Mackay, Charles. *Extraordinary Popular Delusions and the Madness of Crowds.* Boston: L. C. Page & Co., 1932.
> This book, first published in 1841, is a landmark in the study of strange beliefs.

Podmore, Frank. *Mediums of the Nineteenth Century.* 2 Vols. New York: University Books, 1963.
> A reissue of the most complete and intelligent study of early spiritualism ever written.

Pratt, Joseph Gather. *Parapsychology, An Insider's View of ESP.* New York: E. P. Dutton & Co., 1966.
> Gives an insider's view of poltergeists and other psychic phenomena, as well as ESP.

Prince, Walter Franklin. *Noted Witnesses for Psychic Occurrences.* New York: University Books, 1963.
> A collection of strange experiences of famous people.

Rawcliffe, D. H. *Illusions and Delusions of the Supernatural and the Occult.* New York: Dover Publications, 1959.
> An explanation of ghosts and other phenomena from a psychologist's point of view.

Robbins, Rossell Hope. *The Encyclopedia of Witchcraft and Demonology.* New York: Crown Publishers, 1959.
> Contains reliable information on early views of poltergeists, ghosts, etc.

Sidgwick, Eleanor Mildred, ed. *Phantasms of the Living.* New York: University Books, 1962.
> An edited and updated version of a collection of strange and possibly psychic events originally collected by Edmund Gurney, Frederic W. H. Myers, and Frank Podmore.

Somerlott, Robert. *"Here Mr. Splitfoot."* New York: The Viking Press, 1971.
> A lively history of spiritualism and allied subjects.

Spence, Lewis. *An Encyclopedia of Occultism.* New York: Dodd, Mead & Company, 1920.

A remarkable collection of strange lore, by a man who believed much of it.

Spraggett, Allan. *The Unexplained.* New York: The New American Library, 1967.

One of the best books by a believer on current occult beliefs.

West, D. J. *Psychical Research Today.* London: Gerald Duckworth Co., 1967.

An experienced psychical researcher gives an excellent and tough-minded survey of the field.

Index

INDEX

181

About the Author

Daniel Cohen is a free-lance science writer and former managing editor of *Science Digest* magazine. His previous books include MYTHS OF THE SPACE AGE, SECRETS FROM ANCIENT GRAVES, THE AGE OF GIANT MAMMALS, MYSTERIOUS PLACES, A MODERN LOOK AT MONSTERS, MASTERS OF THE OCCULT, and TALKING WITH THE ANIMALS. His articles have appeared in numerous publications.

Mr. Cohen is a native of Chicago and holds a degree in journalism from the University of Illinois. He lives with his wife, young daughter, three dogs, and two cats in a converted farmhouse near Monticello in upstate New York.